QUILTCRAFT
New Dimensions
from Past Traditions

QUILTCRAFT
New Dimensions
from Past Traditions

by

Elaine DeLancey

New Century Publishers, Inc.

Library of Congress Cataloging in Publication Data

DeLancey, Elaine.
    Quiltcraft: new dimensions from past traditions.

    1. Quilt Craft—Patterns. I. Title.
TT835.D45   1985   746.46   85-21791
ISBN 0-8329-0391-4

Contents

Acknowledgments

The scope of talent among quilters today has profoundly amazed and influenced me. I am indebted to all those textile artists who have so beautifully expressed their ideas in fabric before me.

Any quilter's spouse deserves credit for endurance. My husband, Willard Shinners, has patiently encouraged my hobby for the past decade.

To my four children I give thanks for their faith. May they some day remember kindly the time I have spent with thread and needle.

To my parents I dedicate this book. I am grateful that they may share in its culmination.

Whenever I teach or appear publicly with my works, I am the richer for what others share with me. This book is as much for such friends as for my family.

I am indebted to all who have assisted me: Bruce Murray, Mike Thomas, and Susan Juanarena for help with the mechanicals, and Jeff Teeter and Tom McGill for photography.

All projects were planned, designed, and made by the author. Assistance with hand quilting was by Mary Nieland and Gertrude Gutchen.

My appreciation also goes to Patricia Walther for her interest and patience.

Elaine

Introduction

Because of the traditional connotation that the word *quilting* conjures up, namely a bedcover, it behooves me to define my medium as multilayered fabric work. In this book I refer to it as *quiltcraft*.

The word *quilt* derives from the Latin *culcita*, which means bed or mattress. Broadly defined, a quilt is composed of layers of fabric with a stuffing or filling held together by hand stitches, tying, or machine.

We are all familiar with the traditional hand quilt comprised of a top and bottom piece with a center of batting held together with tiny hand stitches. A modern phenomenon is the machine quilt, which also contains three layers, sewn by machine.

Some quilts, such as the crazy quilt, are tied. This is made of random pieces sewn together on a cloth and then embroidered. It uses a center of flannel or wool and a backing. All three layers are then tied.

An exception to the layered quilt is the cathedral window, which is a self-finished quilt composed by a folding method. Still other types of quilts exist which vary from the familiar three layers. Puff and yo-yo quilts are contemporary types, and I categorize them as novelty quilts.

Quiltcraft is a book of innovations in traditional techniques as well as some uniquely original adaptations of contemporary methods. The ideas are inspired by quilting, studies in clothing, and art history.

Many of the ideas in this book evolved while I taught creative quilting at a local college. Some were part of my university Master's Degree Show. Still others are similar to patterns I have had published by McCall's Pattern Co. and Craft Course Publishers.

Since excellent books abound on the subject of quilting, I am including only elementary information so that the beginner can share what I feel is important.

I hope that the ideas here will inspire you, like my students, to express your own talent and individuality.

Happy sewing!

Terminology

Appliqué. Method of applying a designed piece onto a fabric back. From the French word *appliquer*, meaning to put or lay on.

Backing. The bottom layer of a quilt.

Batting. The bonded inner layer of a quilt.

Bias. Diagonal line of fabric at 45-degree angle when edges touch extending from one corner to the opposite corner.

Binding. Bias or straight strip of fabric for finishing edges.

Block. Individual grid squares within a quilt.

Borders. A band that surrounds the quilt like a frame.

Comforter. Very thick and smaller than a quilt. Most often tied.

Continuous bias. A technique of cutting bias from a square or rectangular piece of fabric.

Coverlet. Covers the bed only.

Crosswise grain. Direction from selvage to selvage across the fabric.

Fleece. Needle-punched material used as inner layer between fabrics.

Lattice. Strips of fabric that outline and hold blocks together. Also called *sashings*.

Lengthwise grain. Parallels the selvages.

Marking. Drawing of a design on a quilt.

Mitered. A neat way of eliminating bulk at corners.

Selvages. Edge of lengthwise fabric.

Template. A pattern piece around which you trace.

Tied. Method of using yarn or crochet sheen to hold quilt layers together.

Welting. A corded finished edge covered with fabric.

Chapter 1
Design Resources
and Project Ideas

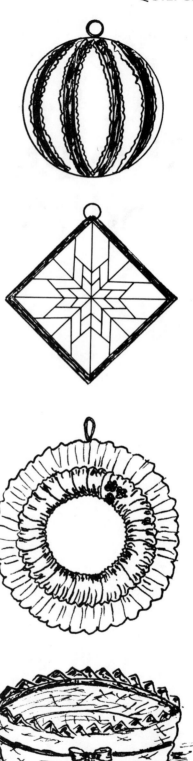

Project Suggestions

- Album covers
- Aprons
- Baby quilts
- Basket linings
- Bibs
- Coats
- Doll quilts
- Dresses
- Hoop pieces
- Jackets
- Miniatures
- Mobiles
- Ornaments
- Pillows
- Pin cushions
- Potholders
- Quilts
- Skirts
- Table covers
- Tooth Fairy pillows
- Vests
- Wallhangings
- Wedding gowns

Design Resources and Techniques

Designs are all around you, so let your imagination go. Museums, libraries, and universities are great sources of other information. Below is a list of other sources of inspiration that are used by quilt designers today. Many are ethnic or cultural in background. When using historical techniques, consider the appropriate colors and fabrics.

Album quilts. Made up of individual blocks, usually designed by different persons and representing a theme. Commemorative in purpose.

Amish. Religious group with unique quilt colors and quilting habits.

Art nouveau. An art form that arose in the 1890s and used flowing lines and organic forms.

Celtic. An interlacing scrollwork design typical of *The Book of Kells* and illuminated manuscripts of the Bible.

Crazy quilting. Associated with the Victorian period. Uses random shapes held together with embroidery, usually tied, and filled with flannel or wool.

Dagging. Sumerian tradition. A process of cutting slashes upward from the hemline. Appears today in fashion.

German Scherensnitte. A scissor-cutting technique making quaint designs.

Hawaiian. A distinct appliquéd whole-cloth technique of great beauty. Folding and cutting method is used to obtain designs.

Hmong. From the ancient tribal art of China developed by people in Laos, Thailand, and North Vietnam.

Mandala. A symbol of centering used throughout history by many cultures. Refer to the Aztec Calendar Stone from the sixteenth century.

Medallion. An oval or circular shape representing a medal. Designs build from the center outward. Refer to carpet designs.

Miniatures. Small reproductions of designs and techniques.

Mola. Kuna Indian art of the San Blas Islands. Reverse appliqué.

Pennsylvania Dutch (German Dutch). A colorful art from the German settlers of Pennsylvania. This distinct decorative art is not to be confused with that of the Amish.

Rosemalling. Tole painting designs can lend themselves to quilts. A Norwegian folk art using scroll and floral patterns.

Ruching. A pleated, fluted, or gathered strip of fabric, lace, or ribbon used for decoration and trim. Queen Anne period.

Sashiko. A Japanese technique of stitching two fabrics together with small running hand stitches.

Seminole. Florida Indian designs using many small pieces, done today with quick cutting methods.

Slashing. A technique of cutting fabric on the bias in small squares adapted from historical costume. The original intention was to display the many layers of fabrics that one could afford to own. Used in seventeenth-century England.

Trapunto. Raised quilting produced by outlining a pattern area with small single stitches and then padding it with yarn or cotton. Italian quilting utilizes cording for filling channel areas. Shadow quilting uses a sheer fabric over dyed fabric and is also outlined and filled.

Amish   Pennsylvania Dutch   German Scherensnitte

Art Nouveau   Celtic   Rosemalling

Hmong   Slashing   Mandala

Nature   Seminole   Sashiko

The Obvious

If you want to design your own quilt or project but are in doubt about a subject, the obvious may provide something for you. The planning of an album or community quilt often brings out great diversity. The following are subjects contributed by quilters to community projects in my town. The first list is from a city fundraiser for the arts:

1. Tragedy and comedy
2. Embroidered verse, "A Picture Is Worth 1000 Words"
3. Harp
4. Instruments
5. Artist's palette
6. Orchestra conductor
7. Pennsylvania Dutch hex sign of a distelfink
8. Quilters around a quilt
9. Violins
10. Embroidered opera singers
11. Square dancers
12. Ballerina
13. Family singing together
14. Lutes and birds
15. Church

Tragedy and Comedy

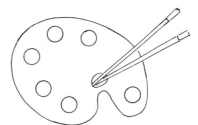

Artist's Palette

The second list is from a project about our town. It includes points of interest, fact and folklore, and history:

1. Owl
2. Pine tree
3. Old church
4. Spider web
5. Old depot
6. Town signs
7. Old schoolhouse
8. Deer
9. Local donkey race
10. Gold nugget
11. Apple tree
12. Mining car
13. Local parade queen

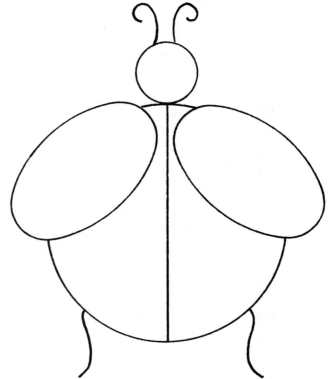

Other ideas may come from nature, magazines, and books. We all have ideas, so keep trying. The obvious may provide your shining hour.

Embroider a web using a twilling stitch for a variation.

Chapter 2
Getting Started:
Join the Crowd

Equipment

Today, the quilt market has a proliferation of tools, equipment, fabrics, and accessories that would astound our forebears. However, in compiling a list of equipment, I remain conservative in the need to use everything. Many hours of work go into a project, and you will want the longest possible life span for each. Who among us does not want to leave something for posterity? Therefore, when selecting fabrics, methods, and materials, consider quality and longevity. Try to understand the effect that various equipment will have on your fabric. Take utmost care concerning the products you use on your fabrics. Time, wear, and chemicals can be detrimental to natural and synthetic fibers.

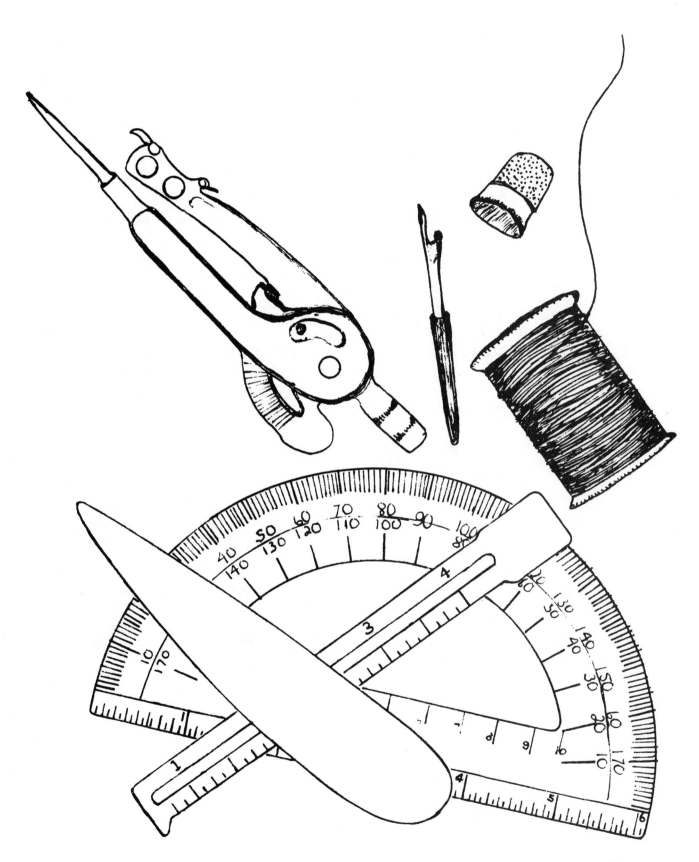

The following is a list of suggested equipment:

Compass. Semicircular designing tool.

Corner poker. To straighten corners when turned.

Graph paper and glue. For cutting designs and making templates.

Manila file holders. These are good for cutting templates.

Pencils. No. 2 or dressmaker pencils for tracing.

Pins, needles. Use both straight seamstress and quilter's betweens. Sharps for basting and hand sewing. Betweens for hand quilting.

Protractor. Necessary tool for designing.

Rulers, gauge. Plastic ruler, a yardstick.

Scissors. Dressmaker shears for fabric cutting, embroidery scissors for appliqué and paper cutting. Always have separate scissors for cutting paper.

Seam ripper. To rip work when necessary.

Thimble. Your size.

Thread. All-purpose can be used, no. 50 mercerized and quilter's thread.

Tracing paper. Dressmaker's paper.

Workboard. I make my own from a product called Celotex which is a white wallboard in 4' by 8' sheets. Have the supplier cut it to size. Cover with muslin. It is good for cutting and layout.

Quilt designing today consists of many variations on geometric shapes. It may help for the creative quilter to be familiar with the names and construction of these forms. In making your own designs, it is imperative to utilize some common drafting tools. These include a protractor, a compass, and various plastic layout tools found in art supply stores.

Geometric Shapes

The *circumference* is the boundary line of the circle.
The *diameter* is the line through the center.
A *quilter's block* refers to a square design.
An *equilateral* triangle has equal sides.
An *ellipse* or *oval* is egg shaped.
The *golden rectangle* is from the Greek. To obtain the proportions, fold a paper in eight equal parts. The fourth division from the top is the line of centering for the golden rectangle. It is close to the Greek division of one-third from the top. Centering on the golden rectangle line gives balance and proportion.
An *isosceles* triangle has two equal sides.
Octagon divisions are obtained easily by following the broken lines.
Hexagon divisions are obtained by using a compass and finding six equal parts.
The *diamond* shape is often used in quilting.

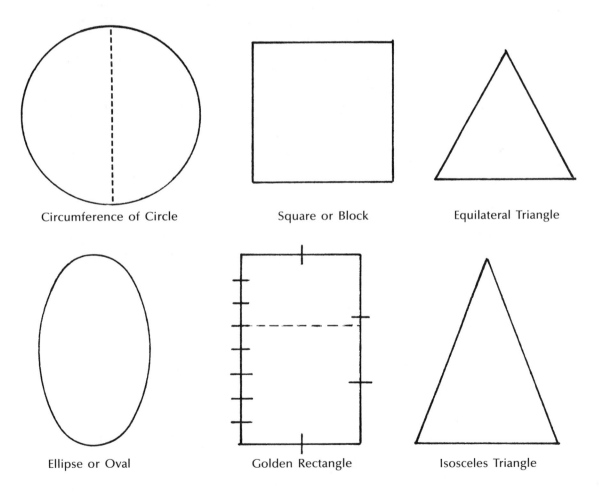

Circumference of Circle   Square or Block   Equilateral Triangle

Ellipse or Oval   Golden Rectangle   Isosceles Triangle

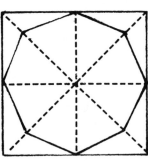

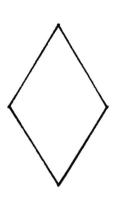

Octagon Divisions   Hexagon Divisions   Diamond

The beginner will be helped in drafting patterns by analyzing the division of a block design. Each design consists of shapes and divisions, from a single square to variations of many triangles and smaller squares.

To construct a block, first study the components of the design. Each division will be drafted, cut, and sewn to form the design. Most important, each piece will require a ¼″ seam before cutting and sewing.

Before cutting a pattern piece, read the directions to ascertain whether or not seams are allowed. Many patterns require the addition of seams while others include them.

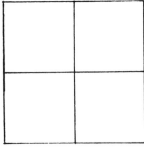
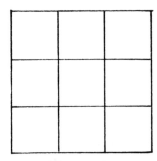

Four-patch   Nine-patch

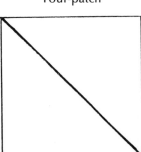
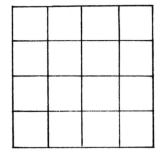

Triangles forming square   Four-patch divided again to form sixteen

Fabric

The type of fabric chosen will be determined by the project. Calico of 100 percent cotton content is best to work with. It folds well and has a good life span. Select quality cotton of medium weight. Prewash before using to remove finishes and allow for shrinkage. Also watch for color bleeding. I have averted some disasters by prewashing and finding the dyes were not set.

Consider the history and appropriateness of your fabric. When doing crazy quilting, you will want to select satins, velvets, and solid fabrics. A wedding piece would require lace, crepe satins, and eyelets. For a baby, choose ginghams, checks, and light prints. Cathedral windows look lovely with muslin and prints. For folded stars, I have used cotton prints, crepe satin, eyelets, and solids. Candlewicking is done on muslin that is not prewashed. Amish quilts are done in solid fabrics with distinct colors. Chintz, crepe satin, or polished cotton can add a sheen to a piece when sparingly distributed among other fabrics. Chintz is appropriate for Baltimore quilts and the Georgian and Chippendale periods. For appliqué, fabrics need medium weight to be opaque. Shadow appliqué requires sheer fabric over another fabric such as batiste.

Color

Color can make or break a project. While it is true that early quilts were of necessity made of random scraps, today we have a wide choice of fabrics and colors. It behooves us to select carefully. Often, a beautifully executed quilt is destroyed by cheap fabrics or wrong colors. I would rather wait to find the appropriate fabrics than start and find my work does not satisfy my aesthetic senses.

People frequently comment on my color selection. They assume it is something that just naturally occurs. Actually, I take much painstaking time to select the colors and prints. It is wise to try a small project such as a pillow first to see what the effect might be before purchasing all of the fabric for a quilt. Conversely, be sure that you purchase enough fabric to finish a project once you have decided. I almost always buy 3½ yards of a fabric if I like it and think I might use it in a quilt.

It is a good habit to cut swatches and place them adjacent to each other for study. Set them out on a piece of paper and look at them frequently during the week. Different lighting may change how you feel about them.

With the high cost of fabrics, watch for sales and plan ahead. Take your patterns to the shop and buy coordinating prints. Plan ahead, considering where, how, and for whom your project will be made. It takes time to select fabrics. Do not wait for a class to meet and then pick up fabric. Take time to prewash fabrics.

If your eye gravitates to a particular print or color, then build around that as a focal point. Often the prints suggest coordinating pieces of fabric. Make it simple, and when in doubt select solids and prints suggested as coordinating pieces by the fabric company. Look for lights and darks, small and medium prints. Large designs usually do not work well in quilting. Consider design directions on the fabrics. Will they give you problems in cutting or laying out the pattern? Think also about warm and cool shades. Do you want the quilt for an accent piece in a room, or do you want to plan the room around the quilt? Will it be a wallhanging? Quilts today have become art pieces to be hung, as artistic works should be.

If color is intimidating to you, follow some safety rules in color selection:

Analogous colors. Colors that are adjacent on the color wheel. Blend a range of the same color family together. They could go from darks to lights in the same hue.

Complementary colors. Colors opposite each other on the color wheel. This can give striking effects. Red–green, orange–blue, yellow–violet are complementary.

If you still have trouble in selecting fabric, it might be beneficial to evaluate the following:

Hue. The name of a color.
Intensity. The purity of the color.
Value. Darkness or lightness of each color.
Cool color. Blue-green spectrum.
Warm color. Vermilion red.
Primary colors. Red, yellow, and blue.

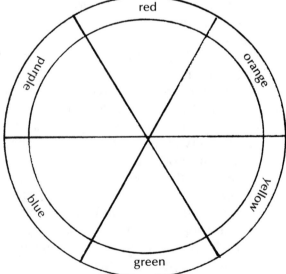

Awareness of the value and intensity of colors helps in selection. Cool and warm colors have a definite effect on a piece. Primary colors are suitable for folk and primitive pieces.

Quilt sizes

To plan a quilt size, start first with the common mattress measurements:

Crib	27" by 52"
Twin	39" by 75"
Double	54" by 75"
Queen	60" by 80"
King	72" by 80"
Super	72" by 84"

To these measurements add pillow tuck of 12" and drops of 10" to the sides and end. This gives a basic plan for the quilt size.

Batting for quilts comes in the following sizes:

Crib	48" by 60"
Twin	65" by 97"
Double	80" by 97"
Queen	86" by 102"
King	104" by 102"
Super	120" by 120"

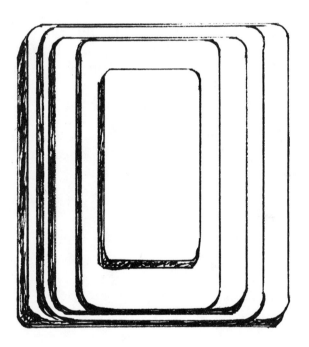

When planning your batting, it should extend beyond the top at least 1" around. Your quilt tuck and drop measurements may vary according to your pillow size and the bed height. A crib quilt will not have a drop. A comforter will require less, being smaller than a quilt. A sham can be used. Quilts can be enlarged easily by adding borders. Waterbeds vary and have no drop. You can also add scallops, a ruffle, or prairie points to the edges to change the size.

Checklist for Success

1. Study and decide on your project size, color, design, fabric, and technique.
2. Choose borders, backing, binding, or other finishing method.
3. Make templates of your pattern. Cut the patterns from graph paper first and glue them onto file folder material. Note whether or not seam allowances are given. Many quilt patterns require you to add the ¼" seam while others include it. A Quilter's Quarter is a handy tool for adding seams.
4. Pin your fabric and pattern pieces onto your celotex board, trace, and cut. Pile in organized groupings according to the block designs. I use a lot of envelopes for small pieces or pin them together.
5. Construct your pieces according to directions. I pin and sew by machine.
6. If you are making a project with sashings or borders, add them by first pinning and then stitching.
7. When your top is completed, proceed with construction of layers where called for by basting the top, batting, and backing together by hand. The type of batting will be determined by the method used. A tied quilt takes a high loft, while a hand-quilted piece requires a low loft. For vests, jackets, and coats I like fleece.
8. To tie or hand quilt, baste your layers every 3" across vertically and horizontally. Next, stretch the work in a frame or put it into a hoop. A pillow may be done in a lap frame. If you do not own a quilt frame, improvise with 1" by 2" boards, c clamps, and wooden stands.

Chapter 3
Traditional Patterns for a Sampler and Wallhangings

This chapter includes the following twelve favorite 14″ designs for a quilt:

1. Pinwheel
2. Card Trick
3. Bowtie
4. Variable Star
5. Bear's Paw
6. Baby Blocks
7. Grandmother's Flower Garden
8. Drunkard's Path Variations
9. Dahlia
10. Clam Shell
11. Grandmother's Fan
12. Dresden Plate

Three Amish designs for wallhangings are also presented:

1. Flying Geese
2. Four Square
3. Triangles

Sampler Quilt

A sampler quilt is a learning project that lets the beginner experience varied techniques. The following designs are some favorites. They are 14″ finished. The quilt sashings are 3″ and the borders are 4″ and 8″ finished. The backing can be made with a queen-sized sheet. Dimensions are 78″ by 94″.

1. Unless noted, the pattern pieces include seam allowances.
2. The designs give a variety of experiences with squares, triangles, and curves.
3. To start, analyze the construction of each block.
4. Trace pattern pieces on manila envelopes, marking the ¼″ seams.
5. Cut fabric, mark seam allowances, and pin pieces together. Baste and sew.
6. Press seams in one direction after sewing each section.
7. Cut nine sashing pieces 3½″ by 14½″.
8. Sew three strips of four blocks and three sashing pieces together vertically.
9. Join the three strips with 3½″ by 65½″ sashings between and on edges.
10. Add 3½″ by 54½″ sashings on top and bottom.
11. Add side borders 10½″ by 71½″. Add top and bottom borders 10½″ by 74½″.
12. Add additional borders according to bed size or choice.
13. Bind the edges. Binding takes 1 yard of fabric.
14. An optional design layout uses corner patches with sashings.
15. Four to six fabric prints and solids are needed.
16. Plan on 3 yards each for borders and block designs.

Sampler layout I. Double size.

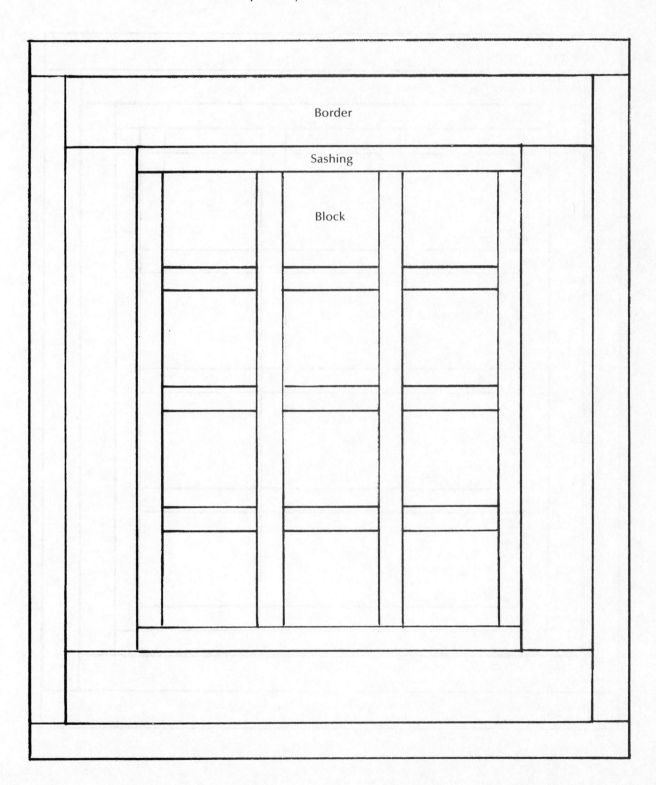

Alternative layout with corner squares. (Uses less fabric.)

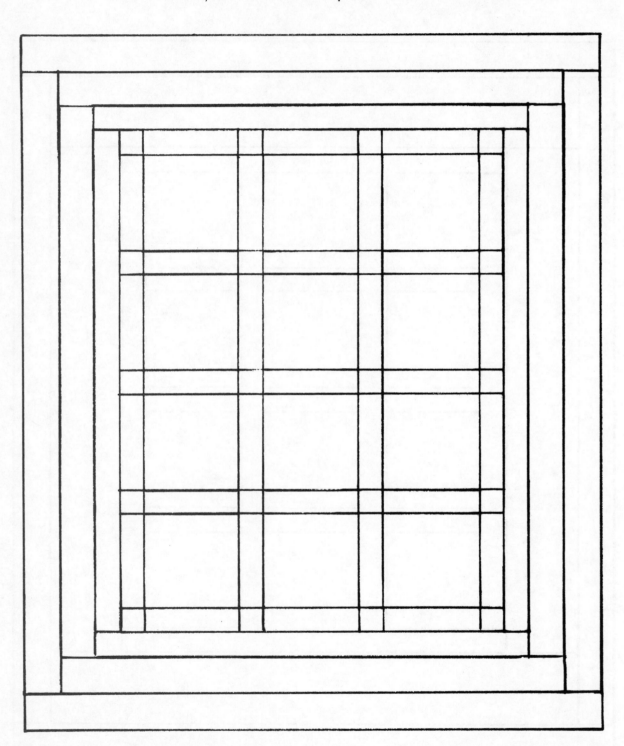

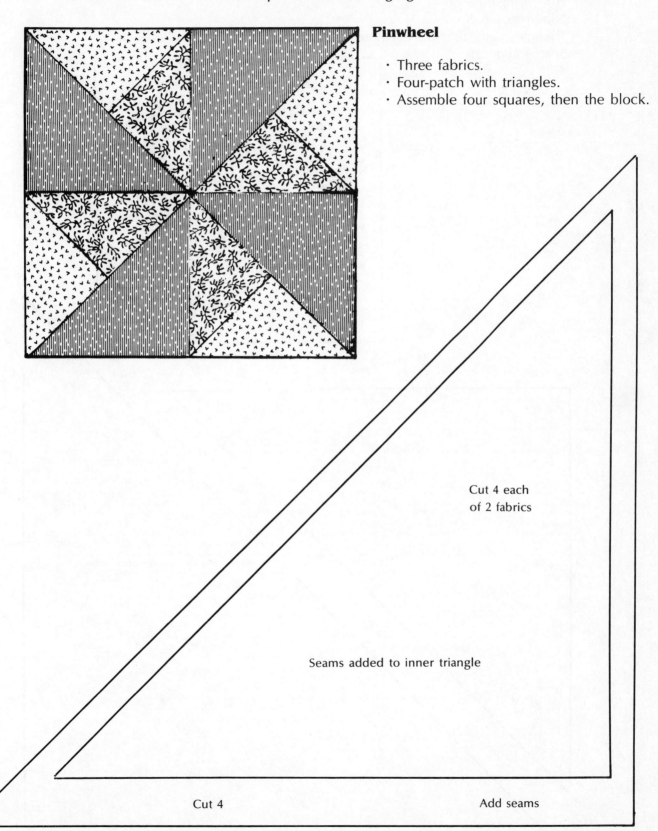

Pinwheel

· Three fabrics.
· Four-patch with triangles.
· Assemble four squares, then the block.

Cut 4 each
of 2 fabrics

Seams added to inner triangle

Cut 4   Add seams

Card Trick

· Four prints, one solid.
· Nine-patch blocks.
· Triangles construction. Assemble nine patches, then the whole block.
· Seams allowed.

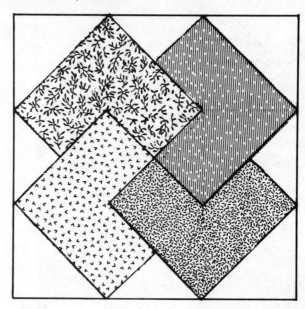

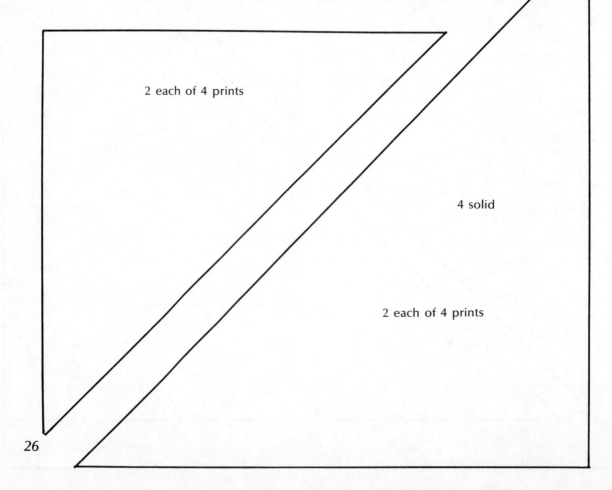

2 each of 4 prints

4 solid

2 each of 4 prints

Bowtie

· Divided four-patch with corner triangles.
· Assemble four patches first.

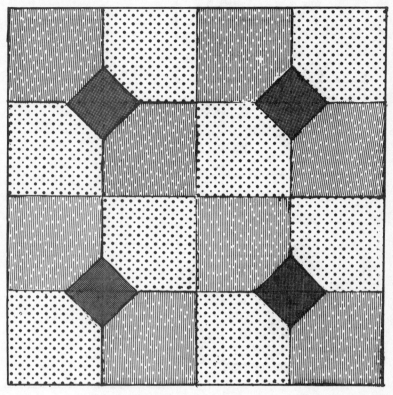

Seams allowed

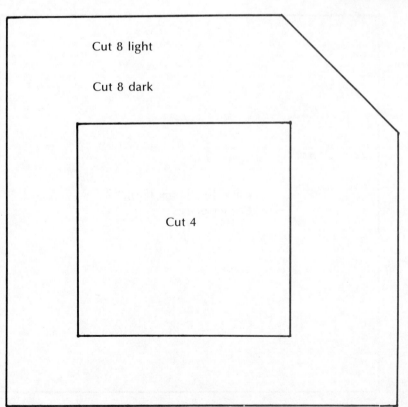

Cut 8 light

Cut 8 dark

Cut 4

27

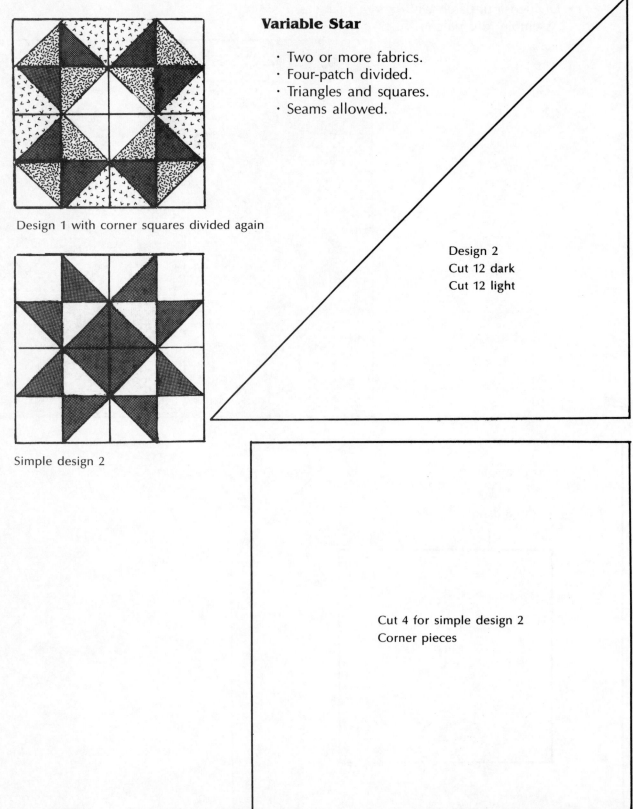

Design 1 with corner squares divided again

Variable Star

· Two or more fabrics.
· Four-patch divided.
· Triangles and squares.
· Seams allowed.

Design 2
Cut 12 dark
Cut 12 light

Simple design 2

Cut 4 for simple design 2
Corner pieces

Bear's Paw

- Three fabrics.
- Triangles and squares.
- Four-patch with strips.

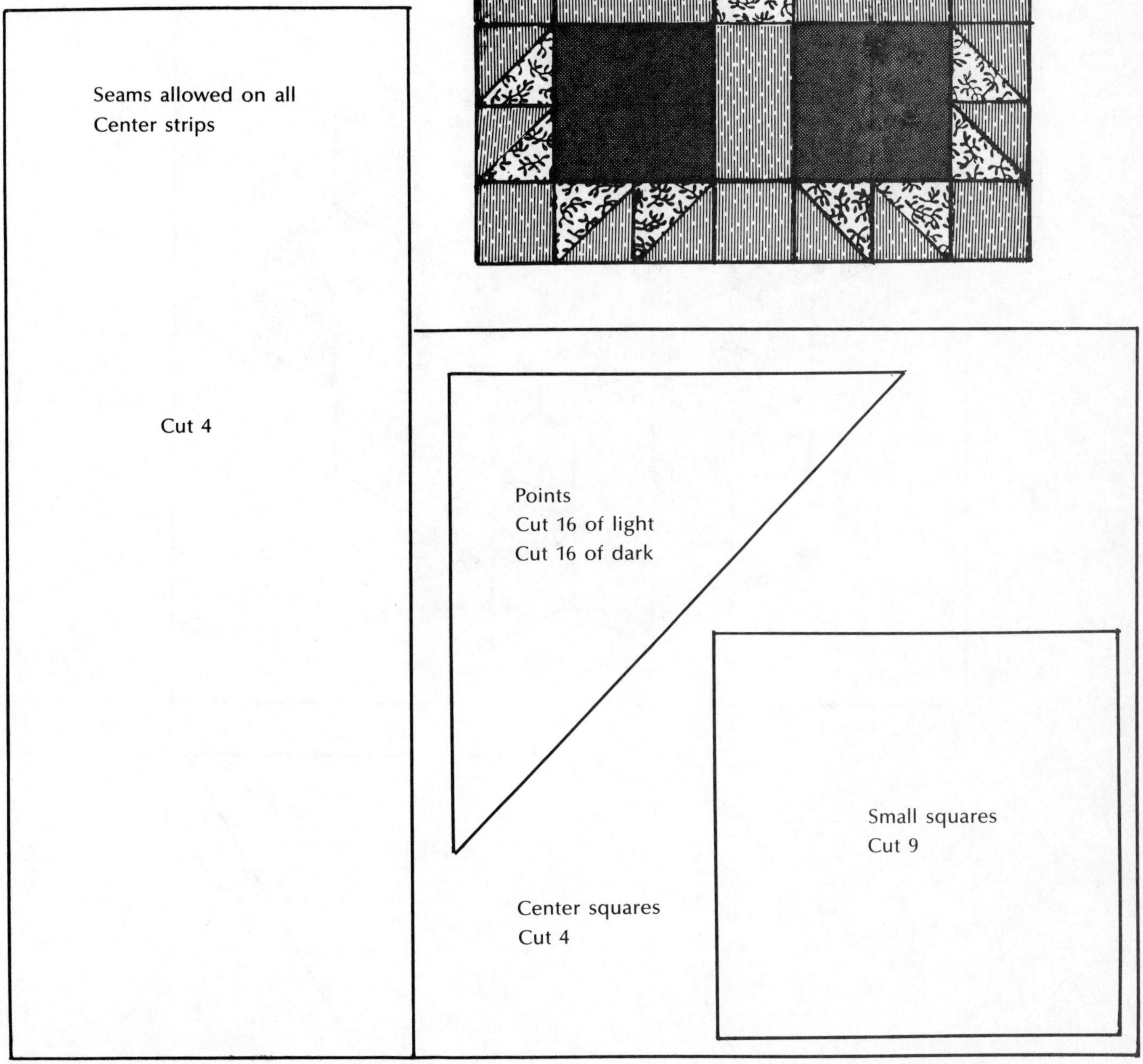

Seams allowed on all
Center strips

Cut 4

Points
Cut 16 of light
Cut 16 of dark

Small squares
Cut 9

Center squares
Cut 4

Baby Blocks

· Appliquéd on backing fabric.
· Three triangles form each block.
· Use of dark, light, and medium fabrics gives optical illusions.

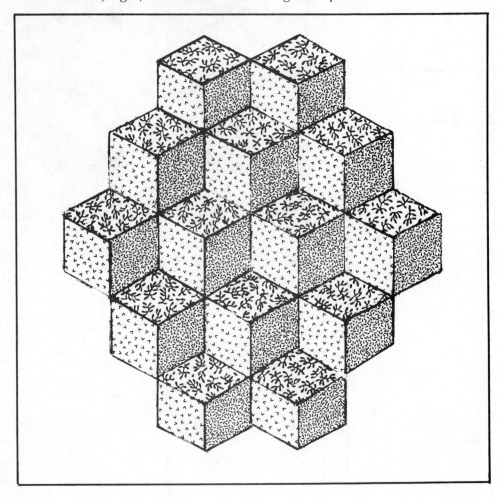

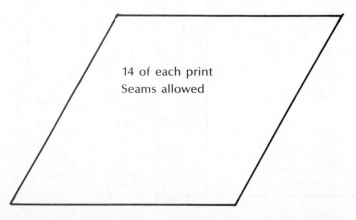

14 of each print
Seams allowed

Grandmother's Flower Garden

- · Hexagons.
- · Appliquéd on block.
- · Two prints, one solid.

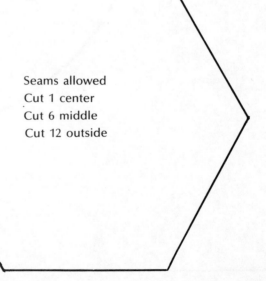

Seams allowed
Cut 1 center
Cut 6 middle
Cut 12 outside

Drunkard's Path Variations

· Four-patch divided.
· Curved and straight edges.
· Seams allowed.

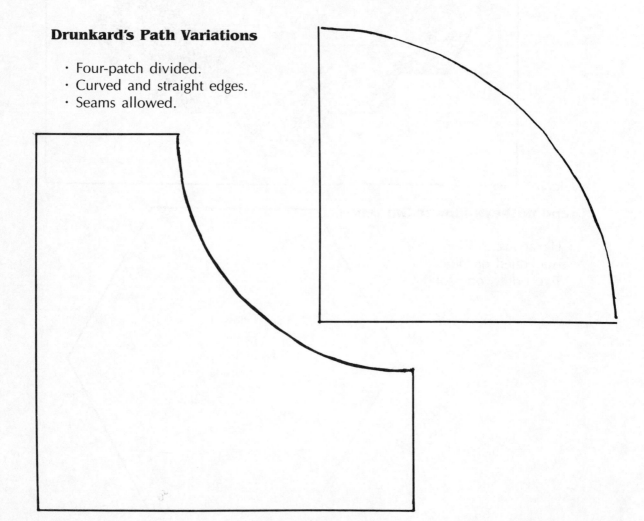

Dahlia

- · Four prints.
- · Appliquéd on backing piece.
- · Center circle.
- · Oval pieces with curved edges.

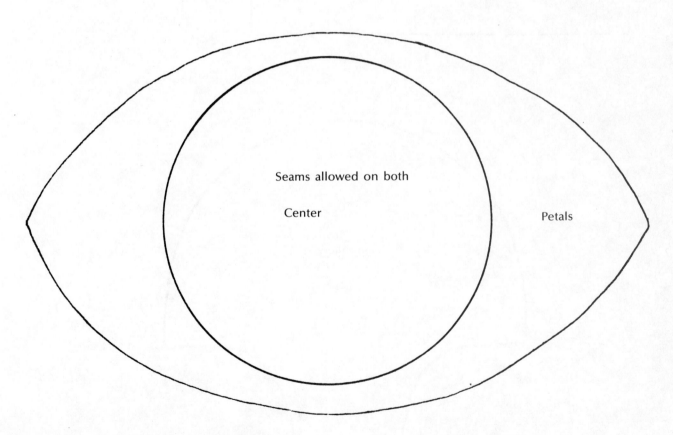

Seams allowed on both

Center

Petals

Clam Shell

· Various prints.
· Appliquéd on backing.
· Curved edges.

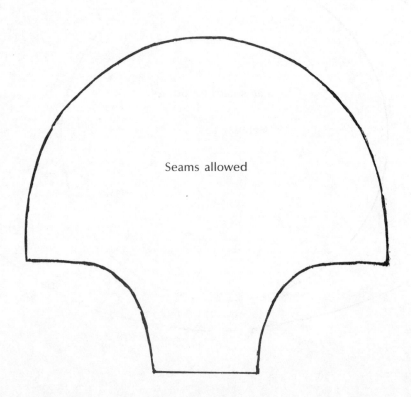

Seams allowed

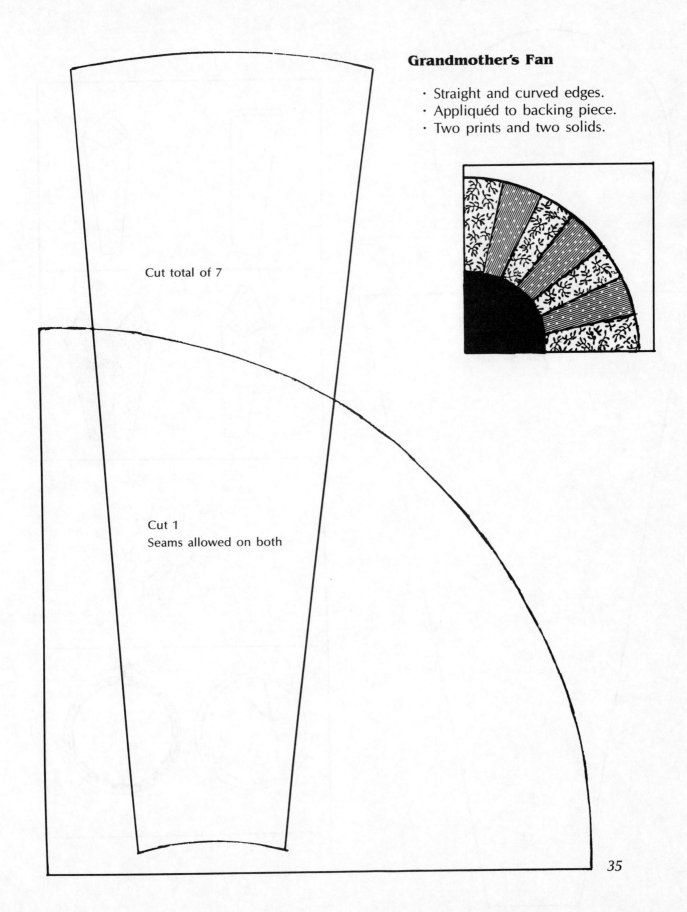

Grandmother's Fan

· Straight and curved edges.
· Appliquéd to backing piece.
· Two prints and two solids.

Cut total of 7

Cut 1
Seams allowed on both

35

Dresden Plate

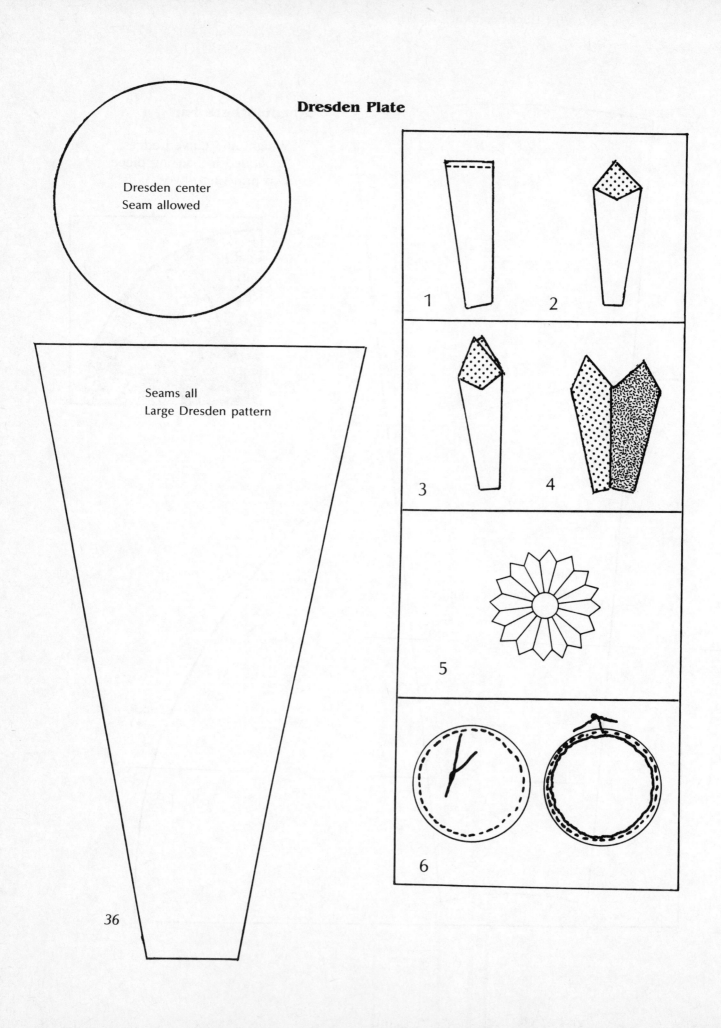

Dresden center
Seam allowed

Seams all
Large Dresden pattern

1

2

3

4

5

6

36

Wallhangings

Amish Flying Geese

- 24" by 28".
- Cut 60 black triangles.
- Cut 120 light triangles.
- Assemble vertical strips.
- Edge with ½" black strips of fabric.
- Assemble with five 1½" by 21" sashings vertically and 1½" by 19½" sashings at top and bottom.
- Add black borders 3" by 19¼" at top and bottom.
- Add black borders 3" by 28" at sides.
- Used tie-dyed fabric for variation.

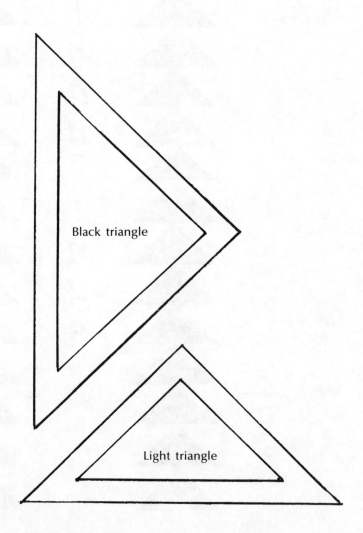

Flying Geese Wallhanging

Amish Four Square

- 22" by 28".
- Cut twenty-four 2½" blue squares. Cut twenty triangles for sides and four corner pieces.
- Cut seventy 1½" black squares.
- Cut seventy 1½" squares of hand-dyed fabrics.
- Cut four light 2" border corner squares.
- Cut two border strips 2" by 20½".
- Cut two border strips 2" by 14½".
- Cut two border strips 3½" by 23½".
- Cut two border strips 3½" by 22".
- Backing 22" by 28".

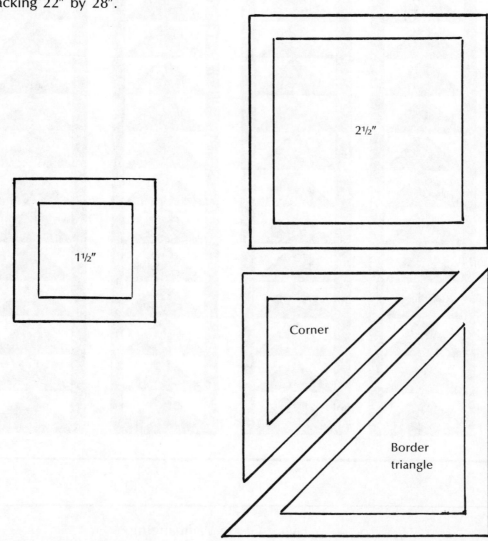

Amish Four Square

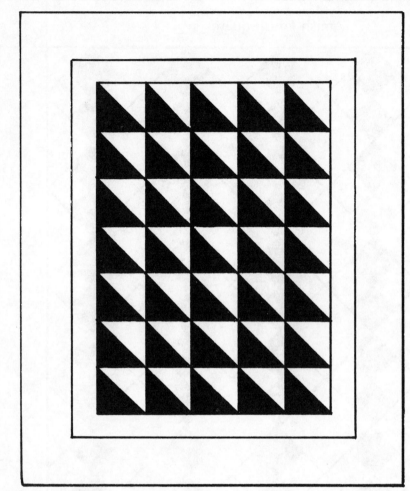

Amish Triangles

· 23″ by 28″.
· Use tie-dyed fabrics.

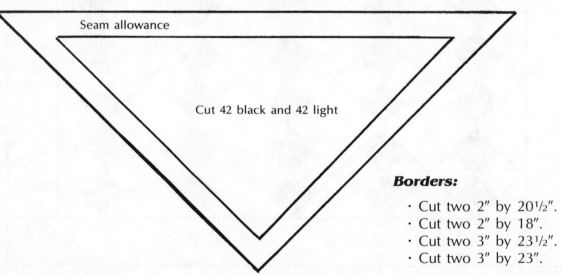

Seam allowance

Cut 42 black and 42 light

Borders:

· Cut two 2″ by 20½″.
· Cut two 2″ by 18″.
· Cut two 3″ by 23½″.
· Cut two 3″ by 23″.

Tie-Dye

· 100% cotton fabric.
· Fabric dye.
· Bowl, gloves, tongs, elastic, and string.

Mix dye according to directions. Fold and press fabric into pleats (1). Twist and tie with elastic or string. Dye and dry. Add additional dyes and repeat process.

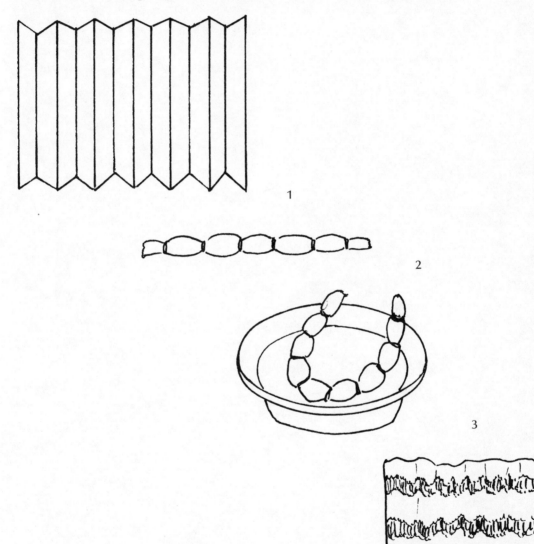

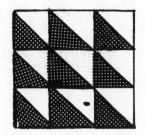  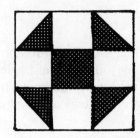

Chapter 4
Small Is Beautiful:
Miniatures

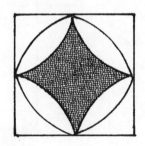 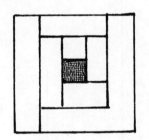

Miniatures are useful and versatile projects for the busy quilter and excellent learning tools for the beginner. Use them to make doll pillows and quilts, sachets, pin cushions, placemats, and table runners and to embellish clothing.

Seven projects are included here:

1. Dresden Plate
2. Log Cabin
3. Folded Star
4. Cathedral Window
5. Shoo Fly
6. Lone Star
7. Ocean Waves

To make a wallhanging, construct twelve 6″ blocks of any pattern. Add to this 2″ sashings and 2″ borders. Completed size is 30″ by 38″.

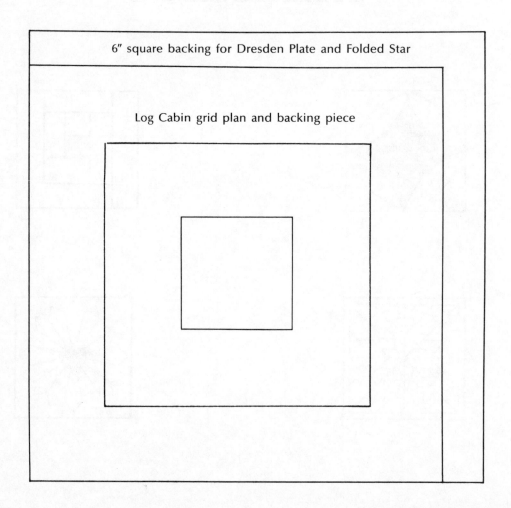

6″ square backing for Dresden Plate and Folded Star

Log Cabin grid plan and backing piece

Dresden Plate

Cut sixteen pieces from the pattern out of scraps. Fold each piece lengthwise in half with right sides together and stitch a ¼" seam across the top. Turn and press seams in one direction.

Repeat until all sixteen are joined.

Cut a center circle from the pattern. Baste around the edge and gather slightly over a paper pattern of the actual finished size. Slip paper out and glue in place adjusting gathers.

Center the petals on a backing piece about 6" square, pin, and slipstitch. Place the center circle over the raw edges and slipstitch.

Add lace to the edge. Sew a backing piece of fabric with right sides together and a ¼" seam leaving space to turn. Stuff and slipstitch opening.

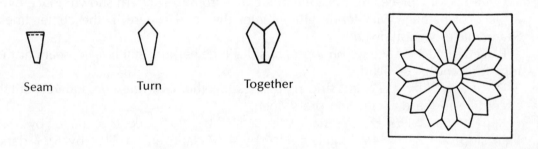

Seam   Turn   Together

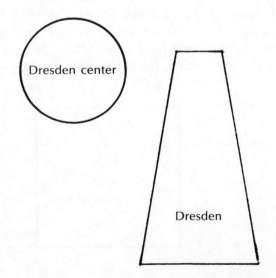

Dresden center

Dresden

Log Cabin

- Fabric scraps, 2 light and 2 dark, and solid center piece.
- 5½" square of muslin backing fabric.
- 6" piece of batting.
- 5½" pillow backing piece.

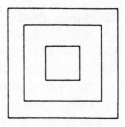

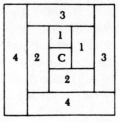

Cut a backing piece and trace the guidelines from the pattern shown. Place over a piece of batting. With fabric glue, center the solid square in the center lines. Seams have been allowed.

Place a light 1½" square on top right sides together and stitch a ¼" seam at the top. Turn and press lightly.

Place a 1½" by 2½" light strip right sides together over the two squares. Stitch according to the diagram and press open.

Repeat with a 1½" by 2½" dark strip, a 1½" by 3½" dark strip, a 1½" by 3½" light strip, a 1½" by 4½" light, a 1½" by 4½" dark, and a 1½" by 5½" dark, clockwise.

You should now have a ladder design across the pillow.

Baste lace to the edges. Place a backing piece with right sides together and stitch leaving an opening for turning. Stuff and slipstitch closed.

Try a miniature doll quilt with the same technique. Make nine squares and sew together a row at a time. Cut 1½" borders to size required and stitch to edges with right sides together and then turning. Cut a backing piece 1" larger all around. Pin in place, tie the quilt, and fold the backing edges in half ½" and then ½" over the quilt raw edge.

Log Cabin
center

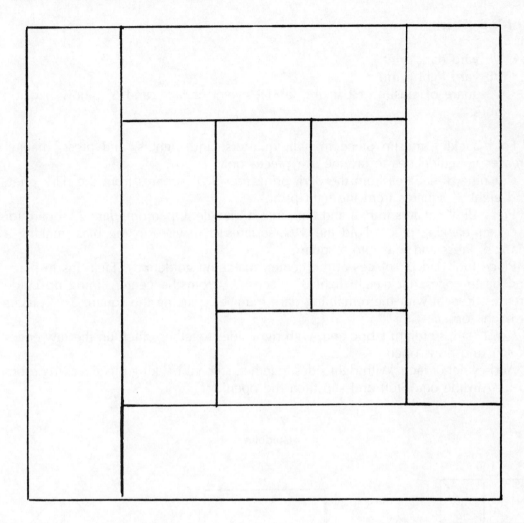

Log Cabin size. For a larger, block, cut wider strips and add another row to each side. Some suggested fabrics for this project are calico, velour, super suede, satin, eyelet, and lace.

Folded Star

- · 1/8 yard dark print.
- · 1/8 yard light print.
- · 6″ square of muslin or backing fabric, eyelet or lace, and 6″ pillow backing fabric.

Fold backing muslin piece in half, quarters, and eighths, and press, making creases for guidelines to lay the star pieces on.

Cut nine 3″ squares from the dark print, four 3½″ squares from the dark print, and eight 3″ squares from the light print.

Press all 3″ squares in half and then into a triangle. Open one dark 3″ square for a center backing piece. Fold the 3½″ squares crosswise on the bias, making a triangle. Press and fold into a square.

Place four dark 3″ pieces at the center, matching guidelines. Tack tips in place and baste edges. Tack eight light 3″ pieces ½″ from the center, lining up guide creases. Repeat with the remaining dark triangles, placing the square 3½″ pieces at each corner.

Cut 1″ strips of light fabric and, with right sides together, stitch on the raw edges of star and press open.

Add eyelet or lace. With right sides together, stitch a backing piece leaving room to turn inside out. Stuff and slipstitch the opening.

Guidelines

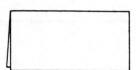
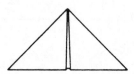

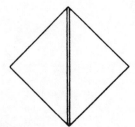

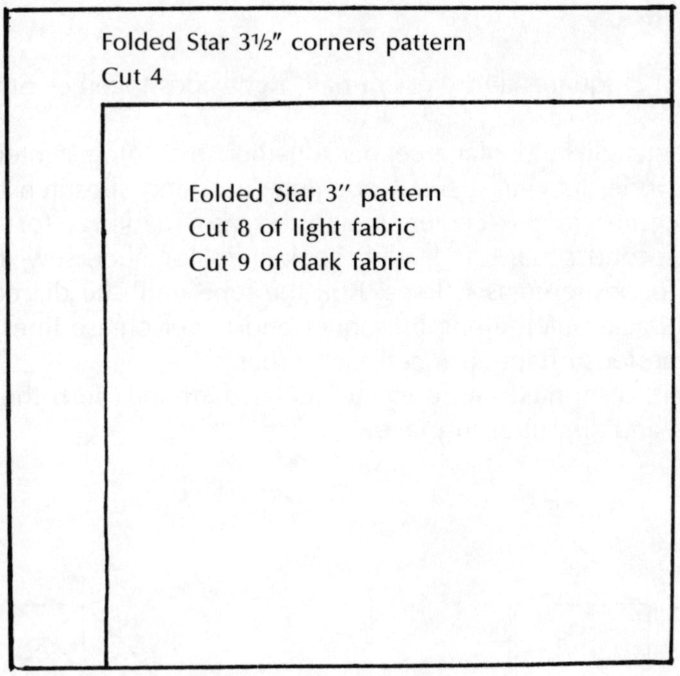

Folded Star 3½″ corners pattern
Cut 4

Folded Star 3″ pattern
Cut 8 of light fabric
Cut 9 of dark fabric

Cathedral Window

Cut two 10″ or 12″ squares and press in half, right sides together. Stitch across ends with ¼″ seams.

Open the rectangle and place seams together, matching centers. Stitch a ¼″ seam on either side, leaving a small opening. Turn and slipstitch the opening.

Press each corner to the center, making crease markings for sewing guides. Complete the second square and, with back sides together, sew the two squares together along opposite creased lines. Roll the tube until the diamond shape is at the center and back. Stitch along the upper and lower crease lines, leaving space to stuff. Fold the loose flaps to meet each other.

Place a square of printed fabric in the center diamond. Turn the flap edges ¼″ over the edges and slipstitch in place.

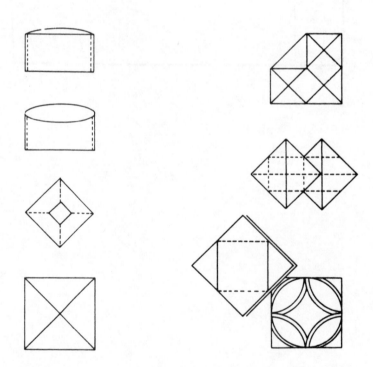

Shoo Fly

Cut four triangles of dark fabric and four of light. With right sides together, stitch the bias edges together, press to one side, and open piece to a square.

Cut one dark center square and four light. With right sides together, sew the top three squares together, then the middle three, and then the lower, and press all seams to one side.

Sew the rows together. Add lace. Sew backing piece, leaving space to turn. Stuff and slipstitch.

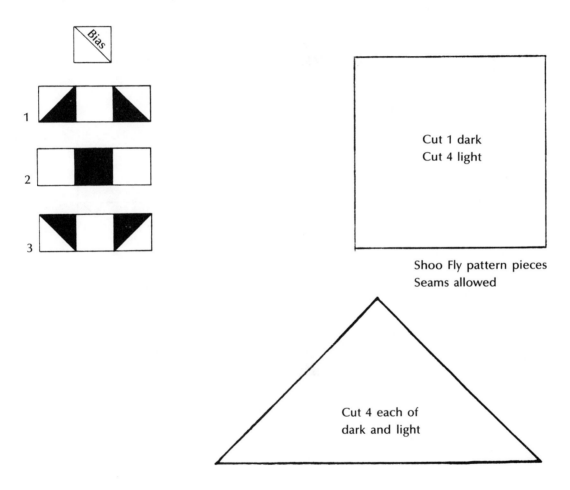

Cut 1 dark
Cut 4 light

Shoo Fly pattern pieces
Seams allowed

Cut 4 each of
dark and light

Shoo Fly
finished guide

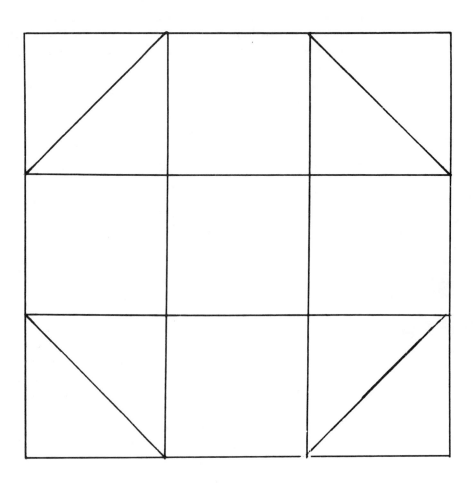

Lone Star and Ocean Waves

For Lone Star:

- Cut one center square of fabric A.
- Cut four corner squares of fabric B.
- Cut four triangles of fabric B.
- Cut four triangles of fabric A.
- Cut eight triangles of fabric C.

For Ocean Waves:

- Cut nine each of a dark and light fabric.

Each of these patterns consists of a nine-patch grid. First assemble individual squares. Combine the squares into rows, and stitch the rows together to form a nine-patch.

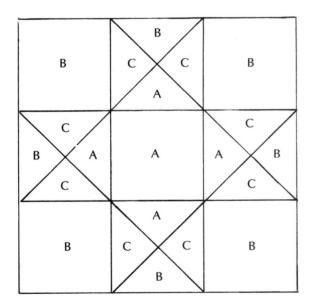

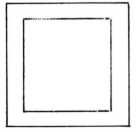

Lone Star

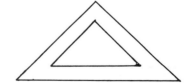

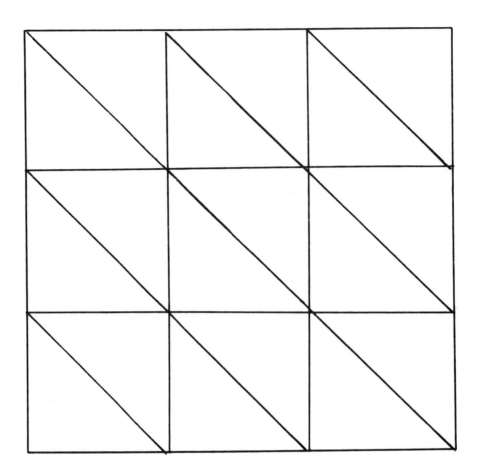

Ocean Waves

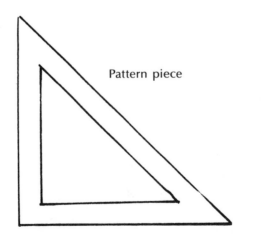

Pattern piece

Chapter 5
Folded Stars:
Everyone Can
Succeed

Since writing my book, *Quilting with Folded Stars*, in 1981, I have continued to experiment with folding fabrics. Some additional techniques are given here, including the English method called Somerset patchwork. It is thought that this folding method appeared among quilters in the United States in the 1930s. However, it resembles the ancient folded fabric works of the Laotian Hmong.

For folding fabric, I find all cotton better than blends. Some patterns shown in this book also include crepe satins, lace, netting, and eyelet. The use of various delicate textures can enhance the project. The wedding pieces are done in monotone shades and rely on variations in texture to accent the star.

Lightweight fabric is best in folding methods. They must be pressed well after folding. Tack points down by hand or stitch through the centers all at once. Fabric glue is helpful in placing points.

Stars are very dimensional and impressive.

Folded Star Square Pillow

Suggested fabrics

Cotton, cotton blends, eyelet, crepe satin, netting, ginghams.

Materials

¾ yard of printed fabric for stars
½ yard of plain fabric for stars
½ yard of muslin for backing of stars
⅓ yard of fabric for continuous bias welting
⅓ to ½ yard of fabric for envelope closure backing to pillows, depending on size
Trims optional

Directions

Prewash all fabrics and trim selvages.

Cut a backing piece for either a 12½" or 14½" pillow (seams allowed). Press the piece in half and quarters, open up, and press to each corner to give guidelines for star placement.

Cut squares as follows:

· The center has five 5" squares.
· Row 2 has eight 5" squares.
· Row 3 has eight 5¾" squares.
· Row 4 has four 5¾" and four 7".

Two folding methods are used. All squares except the 7" are folded in half to make a rectangle and then folded to make a triangle.

The 7" pieces are folded in half to make a triangle and then a square.

To start, open up one folded 5" square and place flat in the center of the backing piece, lining up pressed lines. Place four folded pieces together, lining up pressed and turned lines, and tack the centers in place. Baste or stitch the raw edges in place.

Row 2. Take eight 5" squares and place ¾" from the center, carefully lining up lines. Tack and baste in place.

Row 3. Repeat as for row 2.

Row 4. Repeat the method, placing the square pieces at the corners.

Border pieces are sewn with right sides together on each of opposite sides and pressed open. For a 14" finished pillow cut 2½" strips, and for a 12" finished pillow cut 1½" strips. Sew ¼" seams.

Add lace, eyelet, or continuous bias welting to the edges, basting in place first.

Make an envelope closure backing by cutting either two 12½" by 9" or 14½" by 10" pieces.

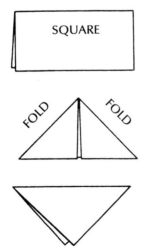

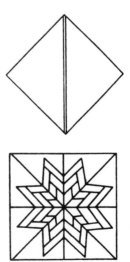

Folded star square pillows are shown in photograph

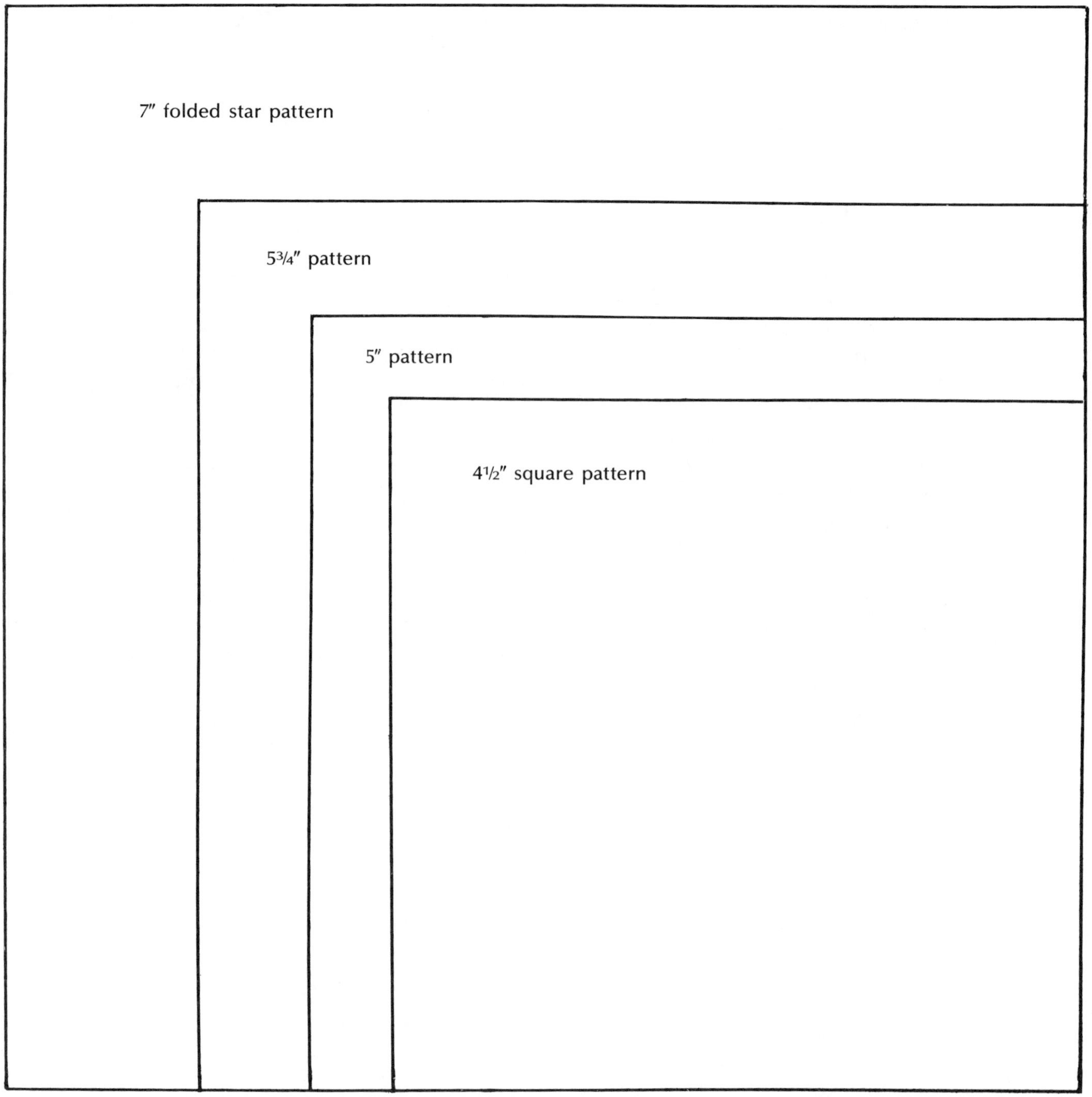

7″ folded star pattern

5¾″ pattern

5″ pattern

4½″ square pattern

Folded Star Bag

The bag is made with the same folded star pattern as the large pillow.

Materials

- Star: As given in pillow pattern
- Bag: 1 yard dark fabric
- Lining: 1 yard light fabric

Directions

1. Make the star.
2. Cut the bag from a piece of fabric 22" by 32½".
3. Make a notch in the middle of each side 1½" by 2".
4. Cut a lining piece the same.
5. Cut one strap 2" by 32¼" from each fabric.
6. Position the star on the front and pin or baste in place.
7. From the light fabric, cut borders for the star, two 2" by 10" and two 2" by 13½".
8. Stitch borders to the top and bottom of the star. Then stitch borders to the sides, continuing to the top of the bag to meet the straps.
9. With right sides together, stitch ⅝" seams on both sides.
10. Match the remaining bottom seams together on each side and stitch.
11. Assemble straps by sewing contrasting pieces together with right sides together. Turn and top stitch.
12. Assemble the lining as with the outside. A pocket inside is optional. With wrong sides together, insert lining into the front bag. Fold the top hem allowances, inserting the straps in place between the bag and the lining. Top stitch the whole top.

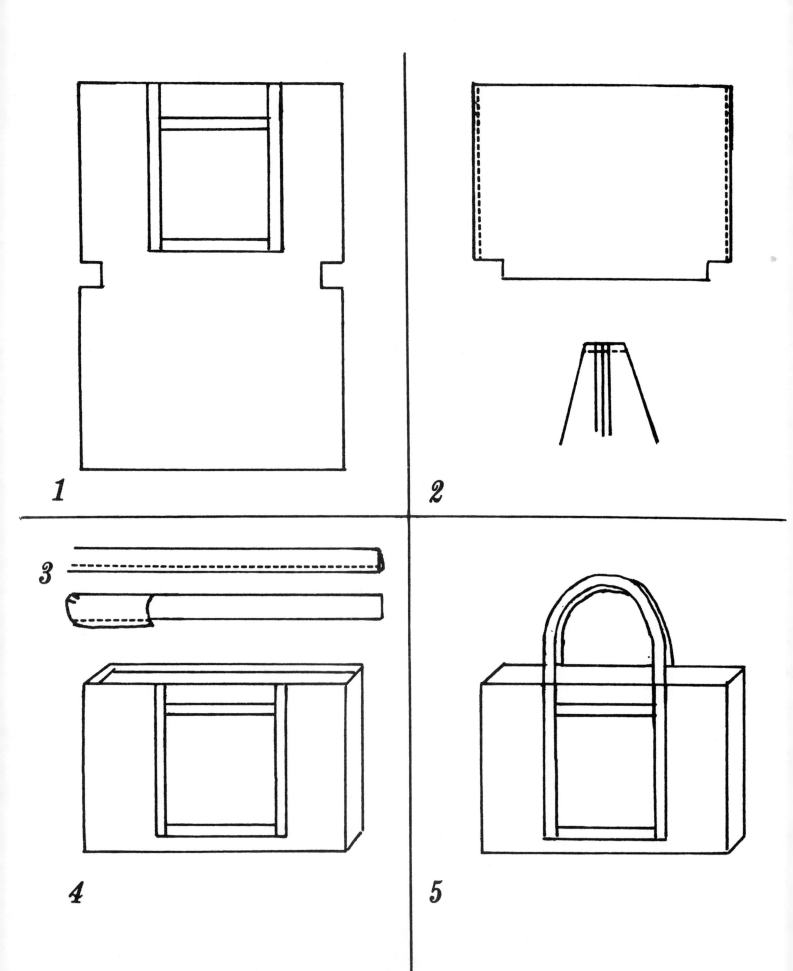

1

2

3

4

5

Folded Star Quilt (74″ by 104″)

Materials

- 1½ yards of muslin for backing of fifteen squares
- 2¼ yards of crepe satin for center stars
- 2¼ yards of netting for second row
- 3 yards of light eyelet for third row
- 2½ yards of printed fabric for borders
- 3 yards of dark eyelet for fourth row
- 3 yards of muslin for sashings and borders

Directions

1. Assemble the blocks as for the pillow on 12½″ backing pieces.
2. Finish the stars with borders of 1″ strips of print.
3. Join the blocks with 3½″ sashings.
4. Add borders of 3½″ wide printed fabric.
5. Add borders of 10″ wide muslin material.
6. Add batting and a backing of muslin.
7. Quilt the sashings and borders.
8. Tie the star centers.

Folded star quilt shown on cover

Folded Star Quilted Vest

Construct the vest back star insert on a 7″ square backing fabric following the star pillow directions.

1. Use three rows of 5″ squares with 6″ corner squares.
2. From muslin, cut a back and front pieces from your favorite vest pattern.
3. Baste the star piece on the back slightly above center.
4. Strip quilt 1″ by 7″ fabric strips horizontally above and below the star, covering the backing area. This is done starting with right sides together at the star, stitching strip seams, and pressing open.
5. Next, strip quilt 1″ strips vertically, filling in the backing areas.
6. At the shoulders, strips are placed horizontally at an angle.
7. Embellish along some seams with lace, ribbon, or braid.
8. Assemble the vest.
9. Construct a lining from the same pattern.
10. Place the lining and finished strip vest with wrong sides together.
11. Baste and bind the edges.
12. Batting or fleece is optional.

Vest done with strip quilting and square folded star piece on back

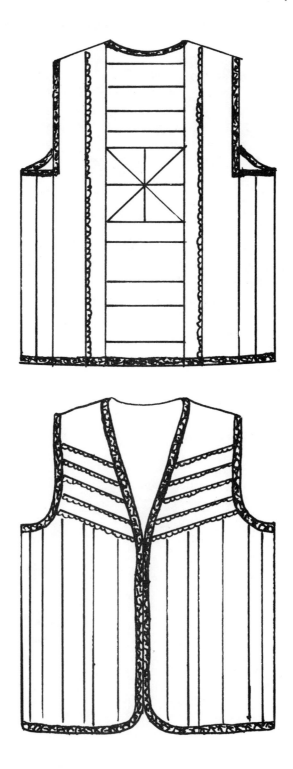

Folded Stars on Coat

The coat matching the bag has small stars on the front as made in the chapter on miniatures.

The back star is the potholder size given under potholders.

The material is polished cotton with a lining and batting sewn by machine. Follow your favorite coat pattern and add stars. Border the star edges with bias.

Pinafore Folded Star

A favorite pattern was used and stars adapted for the bodice.

The border is made of additional folded pieces tacked at the points and finished with a border.

Wedding Dress with Folded Star

Again a favorite pattern was selected and adapted. A star bodice was made and a panel of patchwork added to the skirt. See Chapter 10.

For the bodice stars, use the square potholder pattern directions and add borders. Then continue your commercial pattern directions.

Quilted coat with folded stars used on front and back

Folded Star Round and Square Potholders

Suggested fabrics: 100 percent cotton prints, solids, ginghams.

Materials

For round potholder in two contrasting fabrics:

- ¼ yard of medium-weight fabric for backing piece
- ¼ yard of fabric A (center and row 3)
- ¼ yard of fabric B (contrasting fabric for rows 2 and 4)
- ½ yard of cotton batting (for potholder)
- ¾ yard of doublefold bias (potholder edge)
- 1" curtain ring for hanging

For square potholder or bodice:

- ¼ yard of fabric A
- ⅓ yard of fabric B

Directions for Potholders or Bodice Star

1. For round potholder or coat back, cut an 8" round backing piece.
2. From fabric A cut thirteen 4½" squares for center and row 3.
3. From fabric A cut one 8" circle for finishing potholder back.
4. From fabric B cut sixteen 4½" squares for rows 2 and 4.
5. Cut 8" round circle of batting for potholder.

Follow basic assembly directions as given for the pillow.

1. For square potholder of bodice cut an 8" square backing piece.
2. From fabric A cut thirteen 4½" squares for center and row 3.
3. Cut one 8" square for potholder back.
4. From fabric B cut twelve 4½" squares and four 5½" squares for rows 2 and 4.
5. Fold all as directed in square pillow directions.

Folded Star Wedding Dress

This wedding dress is improvised from a favorite commercial pattern.

The bodice star is from the same fabrics suggested for folded star pillows, namely eyelet, netting, and crepe satin, embellished with lace.

The dress requires 7 yards of eyelet, 3¼ yards of ribbon, 4 yards of eyelet lace, and 1½ yards of gathered eyelet lace for the sleeves.

For the skirt, design a front panel of three varied fabrics. This is easily done by first drafting a paper pattern. From a commercial pattern with a gathered skirt, cut a center panel. Divide it into three sections. Add seam allowances. Then construct the skirt incorporating your front panel. Add lace and ribbon. Add the bottom ruffle.

For the bodice prepare a 7½″ backing piece for the folded star. Follow the assembly directions for the star given under square potholder pattern.

The bodice star is finished with ribbon and a side box-pleat technique in netting. Each box pleat is gathered at the center.

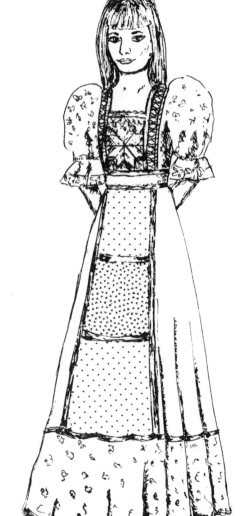

Wedding dress from front cover

Box Pleat

The box pleat can be used in almost any garment as a decorative piece. The wedding dress has a box pleat on either side of the bodice front star. In this garment, the pleats are made from netting. The centers are tied to make a bow effect.

1. For a bodice pleat cut strips 2″ by 80″.
2. Mark cross lines every 1″ and ½″ along the strip.
3. Fold the ½″ lines under the 1″ lines.
4. Pin the folds in place.
5. Stitch along the edges, holding the pleats in place.
6. Take a small stitch in the center of each pleat.

The wedding dress bodice has fifteen tied pleats on each side. Place ribbon along the edges of the pleats.

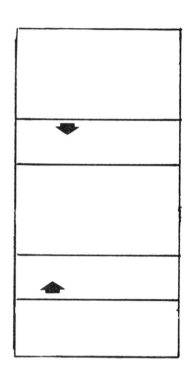

1

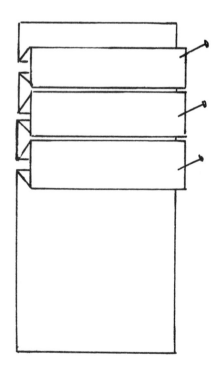

2

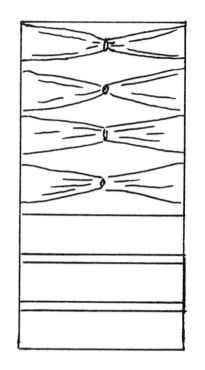

3

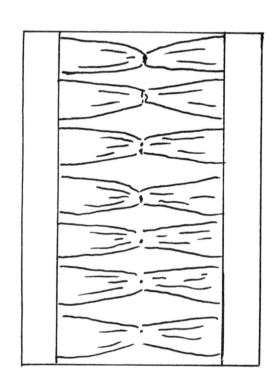

4

Folded Star Pinafore

This is a commercial pattern with the folded star bodice pattern added.
A border of folded points has been added to the skirt.

Somerset Patchwork

The English method of folding a star piece is done with rectangles. It takes less fabric and is less bulky.

There are three rectangle patterns:

- 3″ by 1½″ large
- 2½″ by 1¼″ medium
- 2″ by 1″ small

1. Fold the long edge down along the seam line shown.
2. Fold the corners of the folded edge to the center bottom, making a pie shape.
3. Use the pie shapes as other star patterns with the smallest pieces in the center and the largest on the outside.

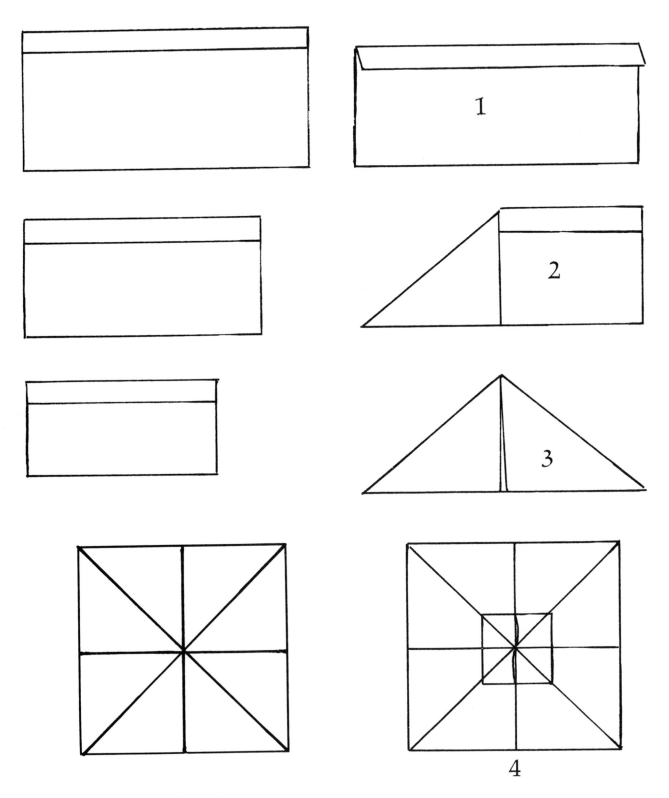

Somerset Patchwork

75

Chapter 6
Cathedral Window:
It Is Easy

Cathedral window is another folding pattern with an obscure history which also may have appeared first in the 1930s. It has evolved through various names and methods. The traditional technique starts with a square; however, innovative quilters have developed patterns made from other shapes such as a six-pointed star or a polygon. These make interesting versions of the design. The construction remains the same: fold the shape in half, stitch two sides, turn, and fold.

The pattern is most often made of muslin, but in my book, *Quilting with Cathedral Window* (1983), I showed a variety of uses for the pattern featuring prints, solids, and other fabrics. For a variation, select unique fabric designs for the window centers, embroider pieces, use photo dye portraits, tie dye, or put lace over solid fabric. For best results in folding, 100 percent cotton is used.

Although the traditional method was done by hand, a quicker contemporary way uses the sewing machine. There is more strength in this assembly method and it is quicker.

While the cathedral window pattern as a quilt requires no batting, backing, or hand quilting, it does take hand sewing to finish it and is just as time consuming. If you are not a hand quilter, you may enjoy this pattern because it is self-finishing and no frame is required to complete it. Once the basic steps are understood, the pattern is very easy to make.

Directions for Cathedral Window Projects

For steps in constructing cathedral windows, refer to Chapter 4 and a miniature pattern. The squares are cut, stitched, turned, and folded as given regardless of the size. Placement of the finished squares will vary according to the project. A square placed at an angle will have windows showing in a different pattern from that of a square placed straight.

Attachment of a square to a backing may be done by machine along the outer flap edges before the finishing work starts. No stitching will be visible when it is done this way.

Remember that the cathedral window is self-finishing and has no raw edges for attaching bias or welting. Therefore, it is easier to plan a project with a backing piece. Stitch the finished windows on the backing and proceed as if there were raw edges to complete seams or ruffle.

Always prewash fabrics, especially muslin. Trim selvage edges. Mark squares carefully along with seam allowances. Press each step of the way. Use a corner poker when turning the squares inside out. Be meticulous for best results.

Cathedral window directions are the same as given in the miniature pattern in Chapter 4.

When combining squares, stitch along the flap fold lines before they are stitched together.

Directions for Diagrams

1. The vest back placement for a square at an angle. Made with four 9" squares and four 2½" windows.
2. Vest front made from five 6" squares and four 1½" chintz windows.
3. Skirt bottom made from eight 18" squares and eight 5" windows.
4. Repeated window pillow pattern made with nine 9" squares and twelve 2½" windows.
5. Photo pillow made with four 16" squares and four 4½" windows.
6. The holiday pinafore follows with a drawing and layout and is made of fifteen 5" squares and ten 1¼" squares. Beads are added between the squares for accent. The pinafore has open sides and is made of both quilted eyelet for the bodice and eyelet fabric for the skirt. The diagram numbered 2 is also the layout for a wallhanging project.
7. A wallhanging made with five 7" squares with children's photos used as the windows.

Both of the photo dye projects are mentioned in Chapter 10.

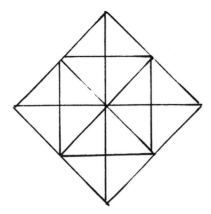

Figure 1 Position of vest back windows with four squares

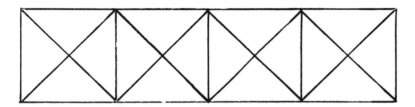

Figure 3 Skirt layout with four squares front and back

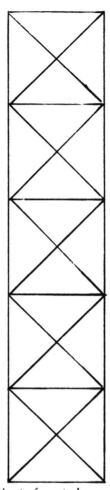

Figure 2 Vest front layout with five squares

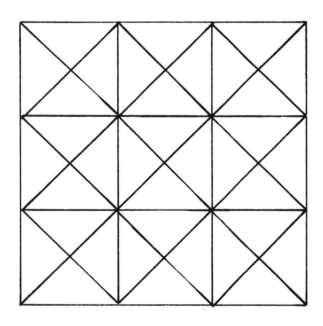

Figure 4 Nine squares for pillow

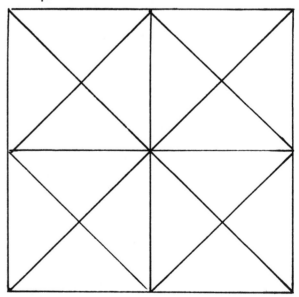

Figure 5 Pillow layout with four squares

Cathedral Window Skirt and Vest

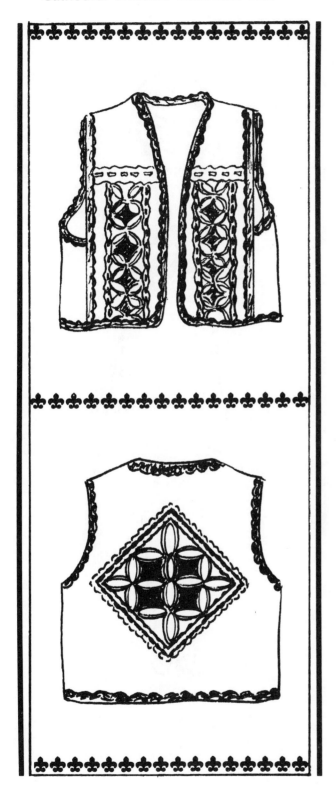

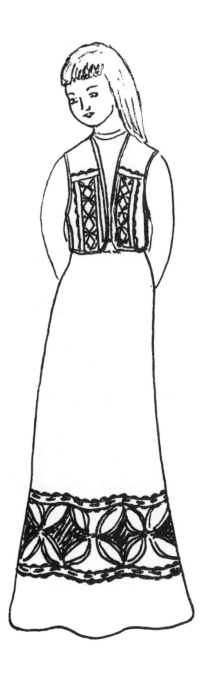

Cathedral Window Christmas Pinafore

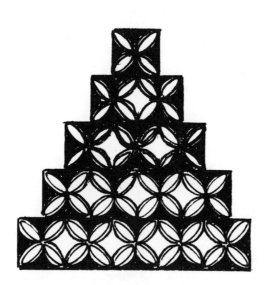

Chapter 7
Magic with Bias
Methods

Ruching Rose

Ruching is a technique that was popular in England centuries ago. It consists of the shirring of ribbon or fabric bias onto a surface fabric. When finished, it has a very dimensional and realistic appearance. When the shirring is done with an undulating stitiching line, a petal effect results.

A quick technique is to shir the ribbon or fabric by machine. Set your sewing machine for a zigzag stitch. Place a piece of crochet sheen thread along the ribbon or bias piece. With the sewing machine set at a basting length stitch, zigzag over the thread, catching the fabric. Stitch one end of the sheen in place and then pull. When the bias is shirred adequately, adhere it to the backing piece. Undo the end of the crochet sheen thread, and pull it through.

Instead of sewing the roses to the backing fabric, a glue gun can be used. The flowers will not come loose.

Materials

- · 1 yard for five roses
- · Scraps of green fabric for stems and leaves
- · Backing fabric for a 14" pillow

The patterns shown have been reduced by 40 percent because of space. The original design was done with 2½" corner squares and a border around the four flowers. The single stem pattern is also reduced. Place a rose on a jacket, a dress, or a soft box.

Directions

1. Trace the rose design onto a 12½" fabric square.
2. Make four bias strips for stems as follows: Fold a 6" square of fabric cross-wise along the bias, press, and open. Mark ¾" lines adjacent to the bias crease and cut. Fold the bias strips, overlapping to form a ¼" stem.

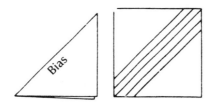

3. Pin or glue the bias strips on the backing piece and slipstitch in place.

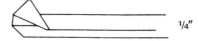

Sampler quilt

Stenciled quilt

Color pictures shown on cover: Folded Star Quilt and Wedding Dress; Folded Star Pillows; Ruching pillow and box; wedding and anniversary albums.

Miniature Pillows

Miniature Log Cabin Doll Quilt

Boy's miniatures on vests

Girl's miniatures on vests

Folded Star Bodice on Wedding Dress

Folded Star on Coat

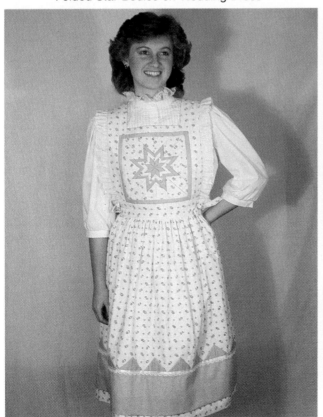

Folded Star Pinafore

Folded Star Bags

9 Square Cathedral Window Pillow

4 Square Cathedral Window Pillows

Cathedral Window Vest and Skirt

Back of Cathedral Window Vest

Appliqued Baby Quilt

Appliqued Country Projects

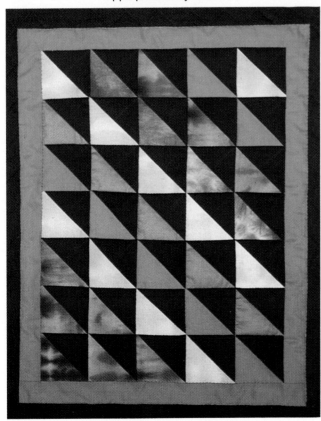

Amish Triangles Wallhanging

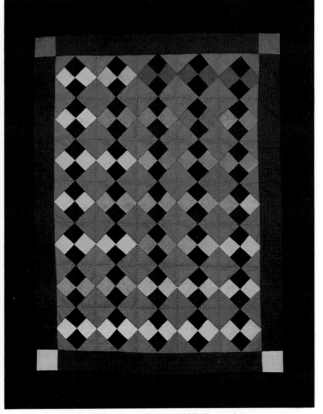

Amish Four-Square Wallhanging

Crazy Quilt Vest

Crazy Quilt Memory Pillow

Embroidered Pillow Vest

String Quilted Dress

Dresden Plate Jacket

Dresden Plate Pinafore

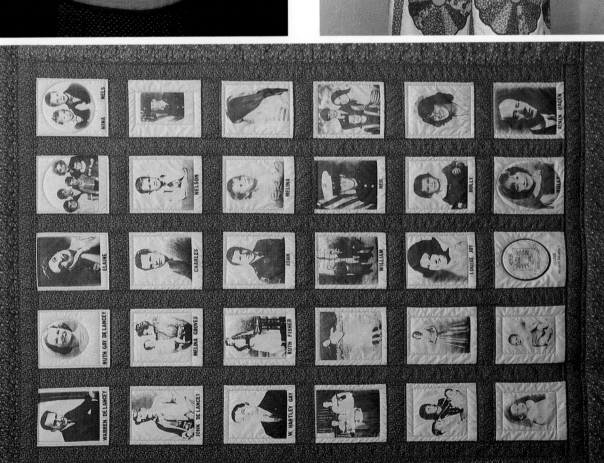

Family Photo Quilt

Christmas Ornaments

Hawaiian and Pineapple Pillows

Puff Pillows in Velour

Baskets

Log Cabin and Pineapple Log Cabin

Log Cabin Pillow in Velour

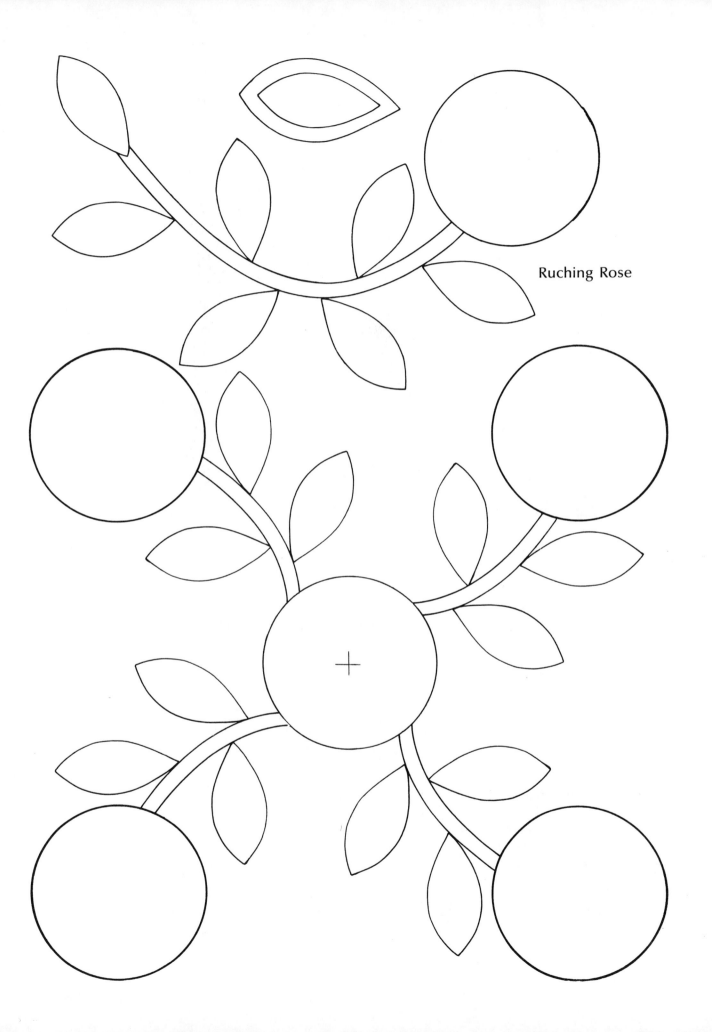

Ruching Rose

3. Pin or glue the bias stips on the backing piece and slipstitch in place.
4. Cut the leaves along added seam allowance. Clip curves and press under the ¼" seam allowances with fabric glue. Pin or glue in place and slipstitch.

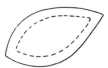

5. For the rose, cut a 14" square of fabric and follow directions for continuous bias, making the strips 2" wide. You will have about 2½ yards. Repeat for each flower. Press the bias wrong sides together to make 1" bias.
6. With a basting stitch on the machine, make scallops every 2". When finished, carefully draw the bias to the desired petal shapes.

Figure 1   Figure 2

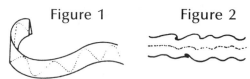

7. Starting at the outside of the drawn petal line, baste and stitch your continuous bias in a spiral, overlapping as you go.
8. At the center, roll the remaining bias strip and tack in place, making a center core. Repeat for the other flowers.

9. To finish the pillow borders, cut four 2½" by 12½" strips. For the corners cut four 2½" squares. With right sides together, stitch the squares to the ends of two strips and press open, with seams in one direction.

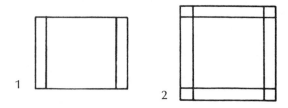

10. Pin the shorter pieces to the raw vertical edges right sides together. Stitch and press open. Repeat with the horizontal pieces, matching seams where the squares meet.
11. Finish the edge with continuous bias welting, lace, or eyelet.
12. Add envelope closure piece right sides together, baste, and stitch. Turn inside out.

Continuous Bias

Continuous bias is used for ruching designs.

Directions

1. Mark a square of fabric from corner to opposite corner on the true bias and cut as indicated by the broken line.
2. Place C & D together to form a parallelogram.
3. With right sides together forming a large tooth, stitch a ¼″ seam at C & D. Open again to a parallelogram and press the seam open.
4. Mark cutting lines according to direction width required. Trim the last small section.
5. Seam the parallelogram together at A & B to form a tube, moving the first line over one line and matching all other lines.
6. Cut continuous bias.

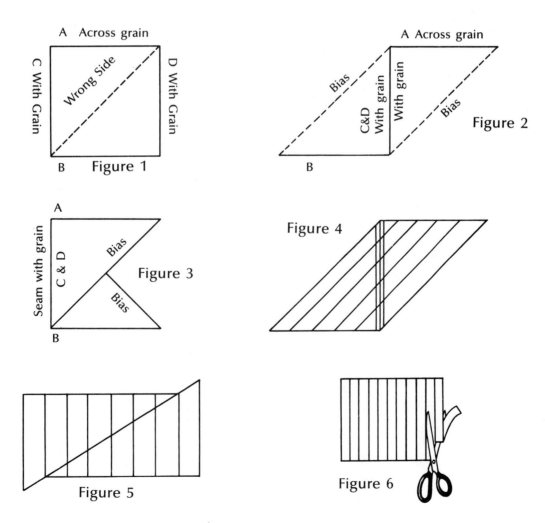

Figure 1

Figure 2

Figure 3

Figure 4

Figure 5

Figure 6

Stained Glass

Stained-glass sewing uses ¼" bias strips cut in the quick method. Designs are reminiscent of stained-glass church windows. Another source of ideas for using this method comes from the flowing lines of art nouveau.

Use solid colors, not prints, for stained-glass design areas. Look for fabrics with slight flecks in them which give the illusion of light. Buy or make black bias for the glass leaded strips.

In assembling, the bias strips end under adjoining strips as they pass over each other. Make window lines overlap design ends.

First, draw a design onto a light background fabric. With fabric glue, place solid fabric pieces in place. Work areas one at a time, placing black bias over design edges and along window design lines. Stitch the bias in place with a blind stitch. Add batting and backing, and hand quilt along the bias lines.

Practice the technique with the tulip design. Use the stained-glass method for a wallhanging, decorate an apron, or make a skirt border. Designs look lovely in a hoop. Look at church windows for additional ideas, or study books on art nouveau.

Stained Glass

Making Bias

Bias for stained-glass or Celtic designs is cut from a square on the bias. Continuous bias is not needed. Short strips are used and overlie each other where they pass.

Directions

1. Cut a square of fabric and fold along the bias from corner to opposite corner. Open flat and mark ¾″ strips parallel to the bias. Cut the strips across using all except the last small pieces.
2. Fold the strips ¼″ on each side toward each other. Fold again in half to make a ¼″ bias.
3. With fabric glue or straight pins, place the bias along the design areas. Cover fabric patch edges. Overlap ends.

Cotton fabrics are easier to work with than polyester and retain a fold line best. Make your own bias; commercial bias tape lacks the necessary color and luster to be attractive. Black is suggested for stained-glass pieces to represent leaded work. For Celtic work, use soft pastel shades in prints or solids to represent ancient manuscript scrollwork.

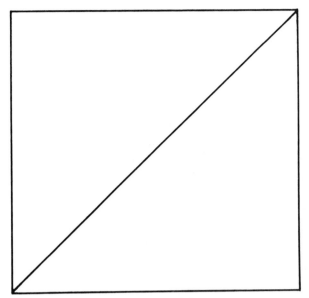

True bias fold

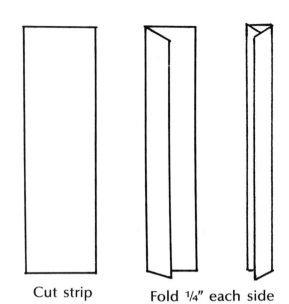

Cut strip   Fold ¼" each side

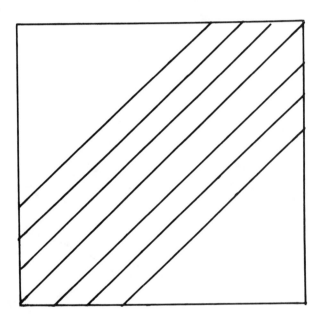

Mark ¾" strips

Butt ends and press or end under
overlapping bias

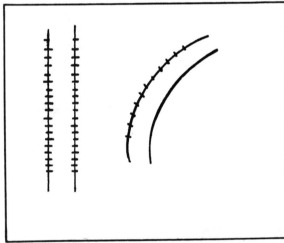

Slipstitch strips in place
Stitch outside curves first

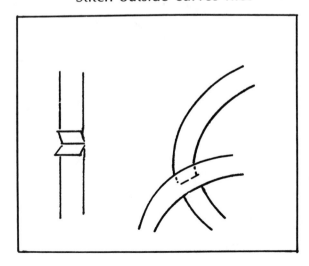

Celtic Designs

Celtic work is representative of the lovely interlacing scrollwork of the ancient monks. The winding embellishments are highly decorative. They are a motif often seen in ancient arts where acanthus and other floral representations were used. Typical of the designs is a constant under and over meandering or interlacing. When making these designs, always check for these repeated changes.

The Celtic designs are made with short rather than continuous bias strips. The bias ends and is covered at points where another strip crosses over it.

Areas enclosed by scrollwork can be filled with fabric patches. The raw edges are covered by the bias. This can give variations to the same pattern design.

For designs, refer to *The Book of Kells*.

Border design

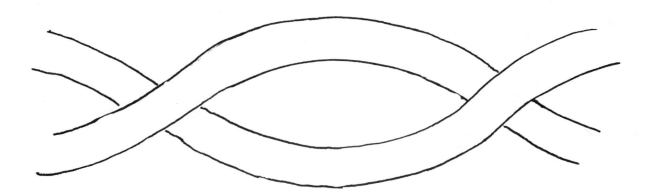

A long tablecloth trimmed with a Celtic design

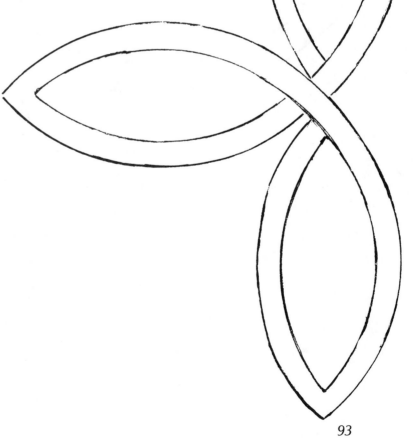

93

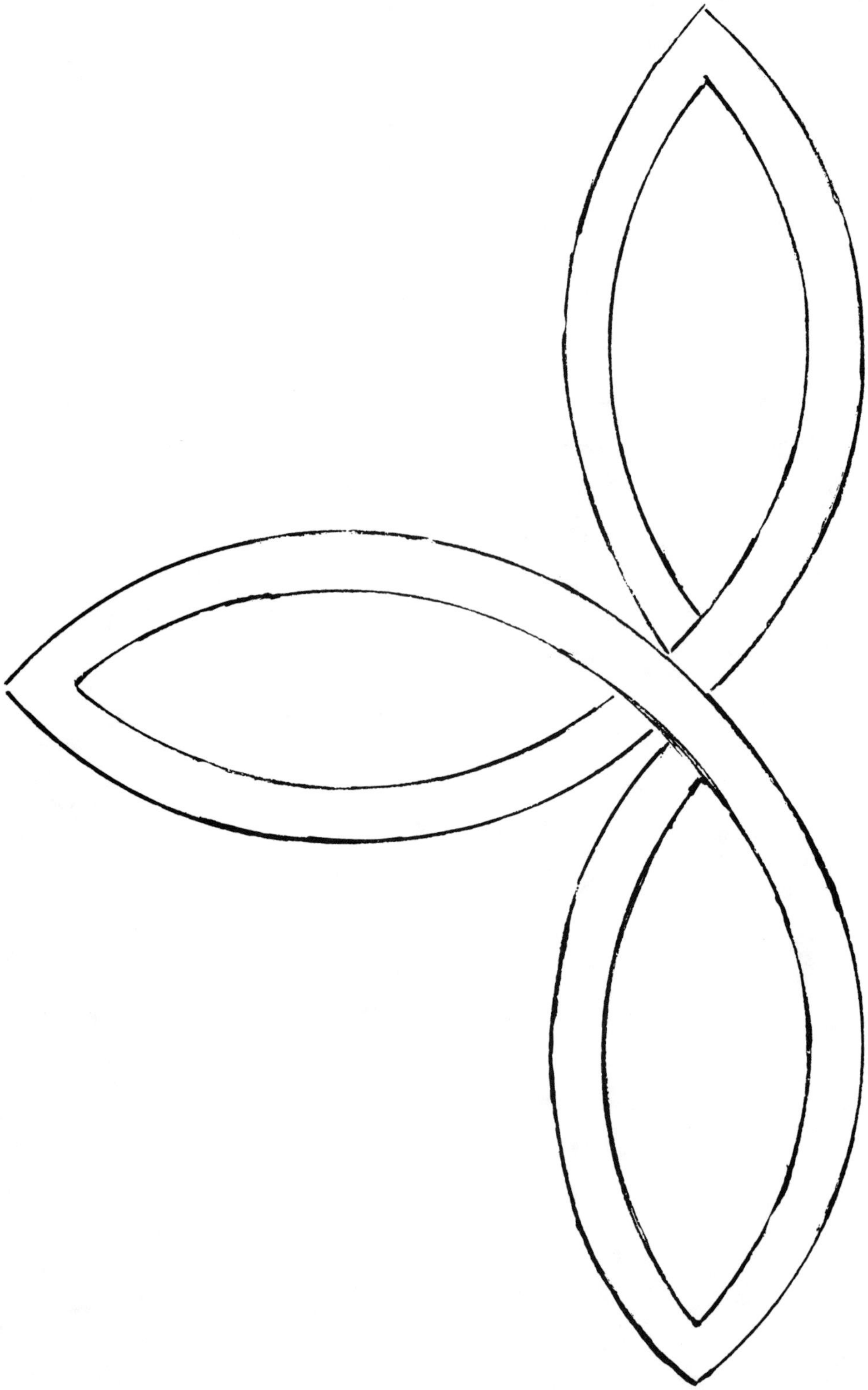

Chapter 8
Appliqué: Country
Tails and More

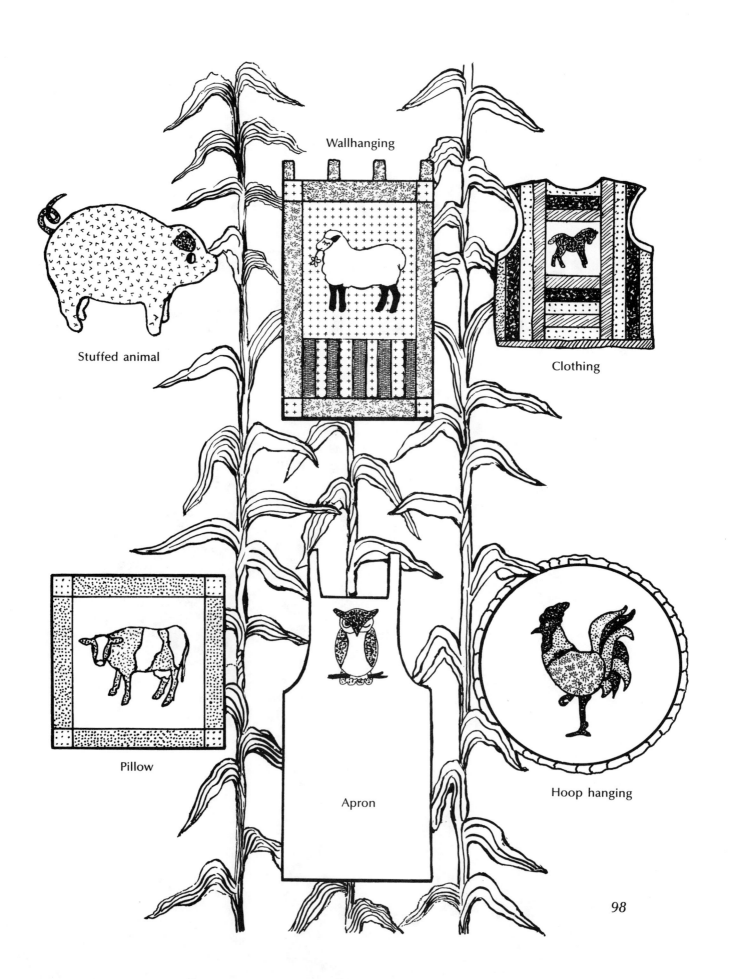

Stuffed animal

Wallhanging

Clothing

Pillow

Apron

Hoop hanging

98

Assembly Suggestions for Appliqué

1. Prewash all fabrics. Read directions through first and select a method.
2. Preserve your patterns by tracing them onto another paper. Lightly mark your full-size design on the backing fabric for placement with dressmaker tracing paper.
3. For machine appliqué no seam allowance is called for. Cut pieces as shown. For other methods, add ¼″ seams as directed.
4. For *machine appliqué*, press iron-on stabilizer to backs of selected fabric pieces. Trace the designs and cut on the lines. Assemble pieces on backing fabric according to numbered sequence. Glue or baste and zigzag each edge with machine satin stitch. (Loosen machine tension.)
5. For *quick appliqué*, pin paper pattern pieces onto selected fabrics and mark the design seam line on the right sides. Cut carefully around, adding a ¼″ seam. Pin each piece in place on the backing fabric and turn under the seam allowances as you go, attaching edges with a slipstitch. Leave seam allowances open and overlap adjacent pieces at broken lines.
6. If pieces are detailed or if you want a *three-dimensional* look, mark seams on the wrong side. Cut two of each piece, allowing a ¼″ seam. With right sides together, stitch all around the pieces. Carefully cut a slit on the back side, remembering that it is to be reversed. Turn inside out and press.
7. Unbonded, low loft batting is preferable for machine appliqué. High loft is nice for the quilts. Plan ahead when buying.
8. To *slipstitch*, work stitches from right to left. Begin by bringing the needle and thread through the turned-under edge from back to front. Form stitches by inserting the needle opposite where it came out. Take small, consistent stitches, about ¼″ apart.

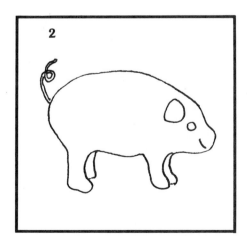
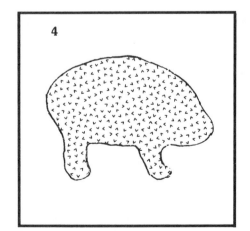

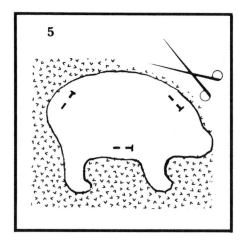
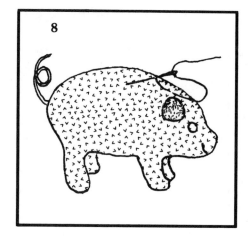

Broken lines on the pattern pieces indicate suggested overlapping where seams are allowed. Create your own markings on the animals if desired. Add hooves; quilt or embroider unique features. Add butterflies and chicks. Refer to the full-size prints for placement of pieces. Use numbering for sequence of piecing with seams.

Baby Farm Quilt (42" by 56")

Materials (all estimates for 44" wide fabric)

· Center appliqués: ½ yard of light print, scraps of dark and solid
· Block fabric for six 12½" squares: ¾ yard
· Sashings (inside strips) and 4½" squares: ¾ yard
· Border B (outside) and 3½" squares: 1 yard
· Backing fabric: 1¾ yard
· Batting: 1¾ yard
· Bias binding: 6 yards
· Iron-on stabilizer (optional)

Directions

1. Prewash all fabrics.
2. Blocks: Cut six 12½" squares for designs.
   Sashings A: Cut seventeen 12½" by 3⅓" strips.
   From contrasting fabric cut twelve 3½" squares.
   Border B: Cut two strips 33½" by 4½". Cut four strips 22½" by 4½".
   From contrasting fabric cut six 4½" squares.
3. Prepare appliqués following general appliqué directions of your choice. Read all first.
4. With *right* sides together, stitch sashing (12½") by 3½" strips to blocks making two rows of three blocks each with four strips each (Figure A).
5. Assemble three rows of side sashings each with four contrasting corner squares and three 12½" by 3½" strips. With right sides together, attach the rows to the block sides, matching the corners carefully. Insert a pin to match (Figure B).
6. Add border B strips (33½" by 4½") to bottom and top with right sides together. Stitch and press open (Figure C).
7. Assemble side borders and squares. With right sides together, attach, sew, and press open (Figure D).
8. Cut a piece of batting and backing 1" larger than the quilt top and baste all three layers together. Hand quilt or tie. Trim the edges even and bind with bias binding.
9. *Hand quilting:* With a needle and no. 50 thread, quilt ¼" around the designs and ¼" each side of the seams. Try marking and quilting original designs. Make stitches even on top and bottom. Bury knots at each end and pull the thread through the batting.
10. *Tie* if preferred. Cut crochet sheen thread about 8" long. With an embroidery needle, sew two stitches in the same two holes through all three layers and tie with a square knot. Repeat every 4".

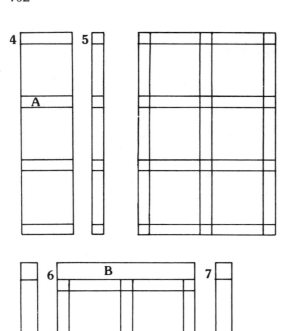

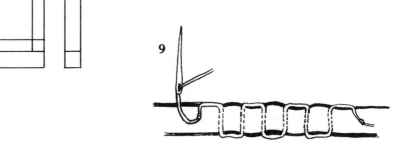

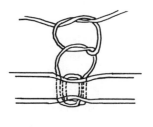

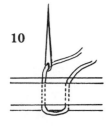

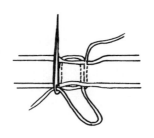

Calico Cat

3

5

2
Cut 2

4

6

1

105

Goosey Gander

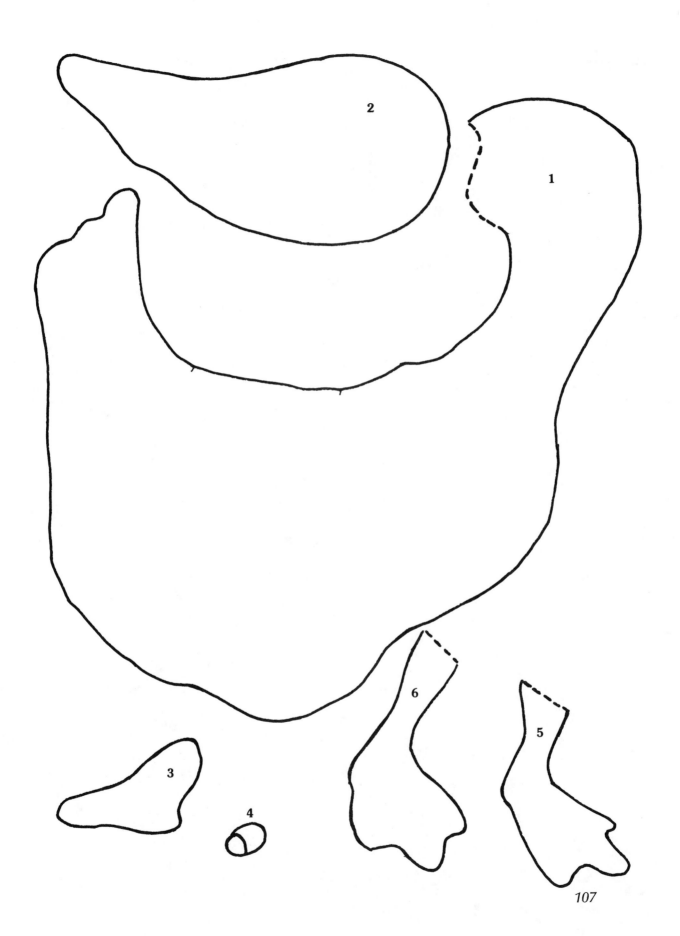

Petunia Pig

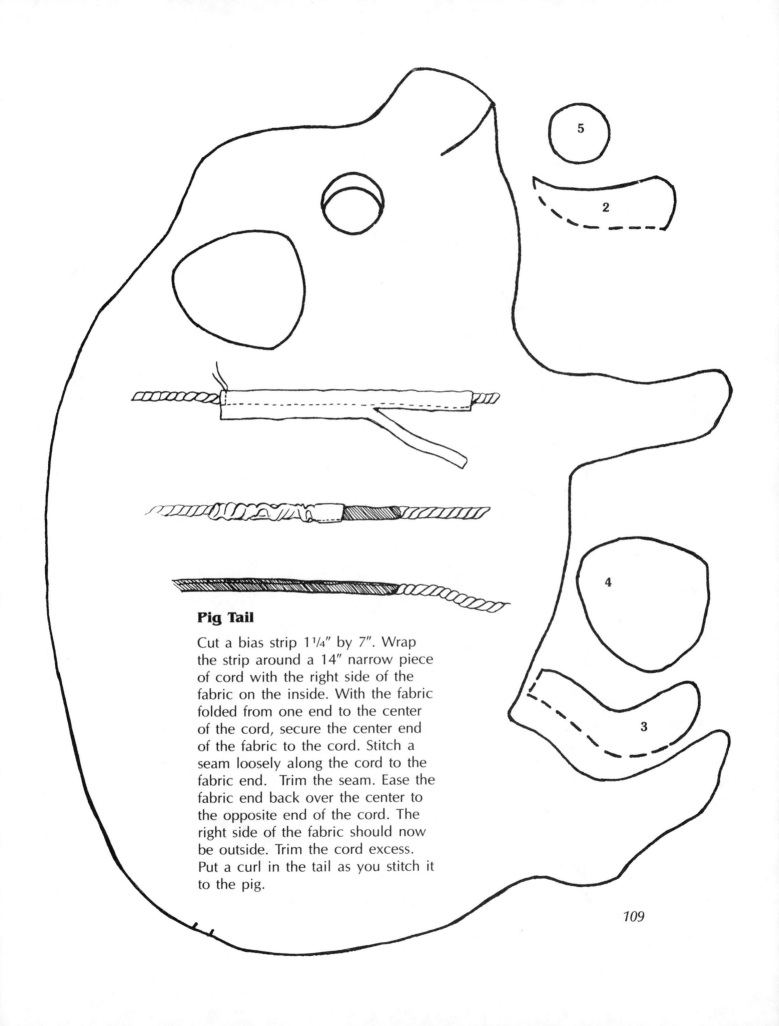

Pig Tail

Cut a bias strip 1¼″ by 7″. Wrap the strip around a 14″ narrow piece of cord with the right side of the fabric on the inside. With the fabric folded from one end to the center of the cord, secure the center end of the fabric to the cord. Stitch a seam loosely along the cord to the fabric end. Trim the seam. Ease the fabric end back over the center to the opposite end of the cord. The right side of the fabric should now be outside. Trim the cord excess. Put a curl in the tail as you stitch it to the pig.

5

2

4

3

Felicia Lamb

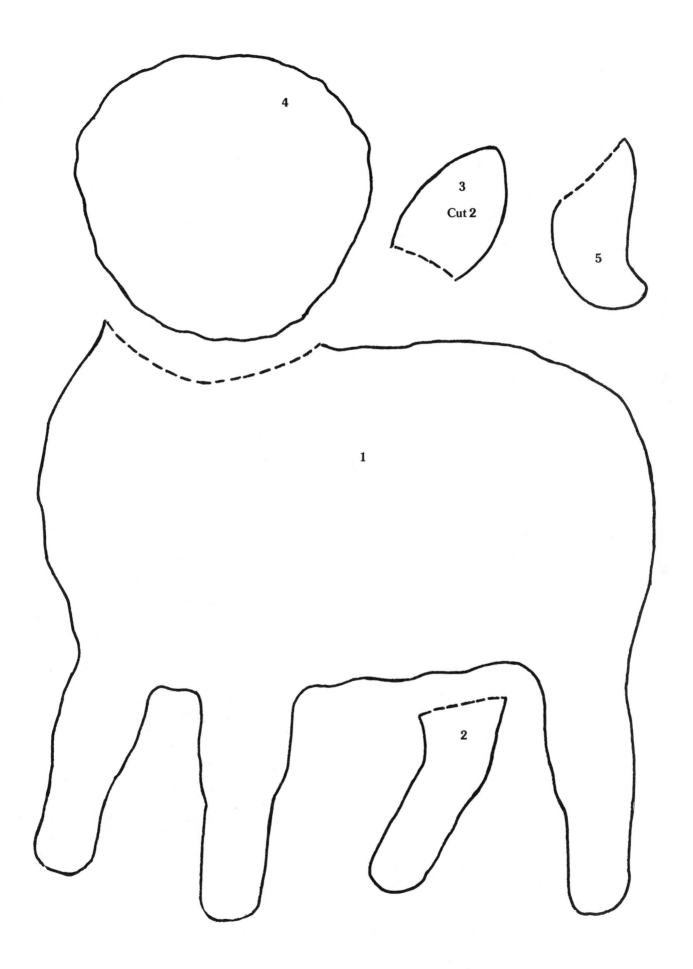

Prancing Pony

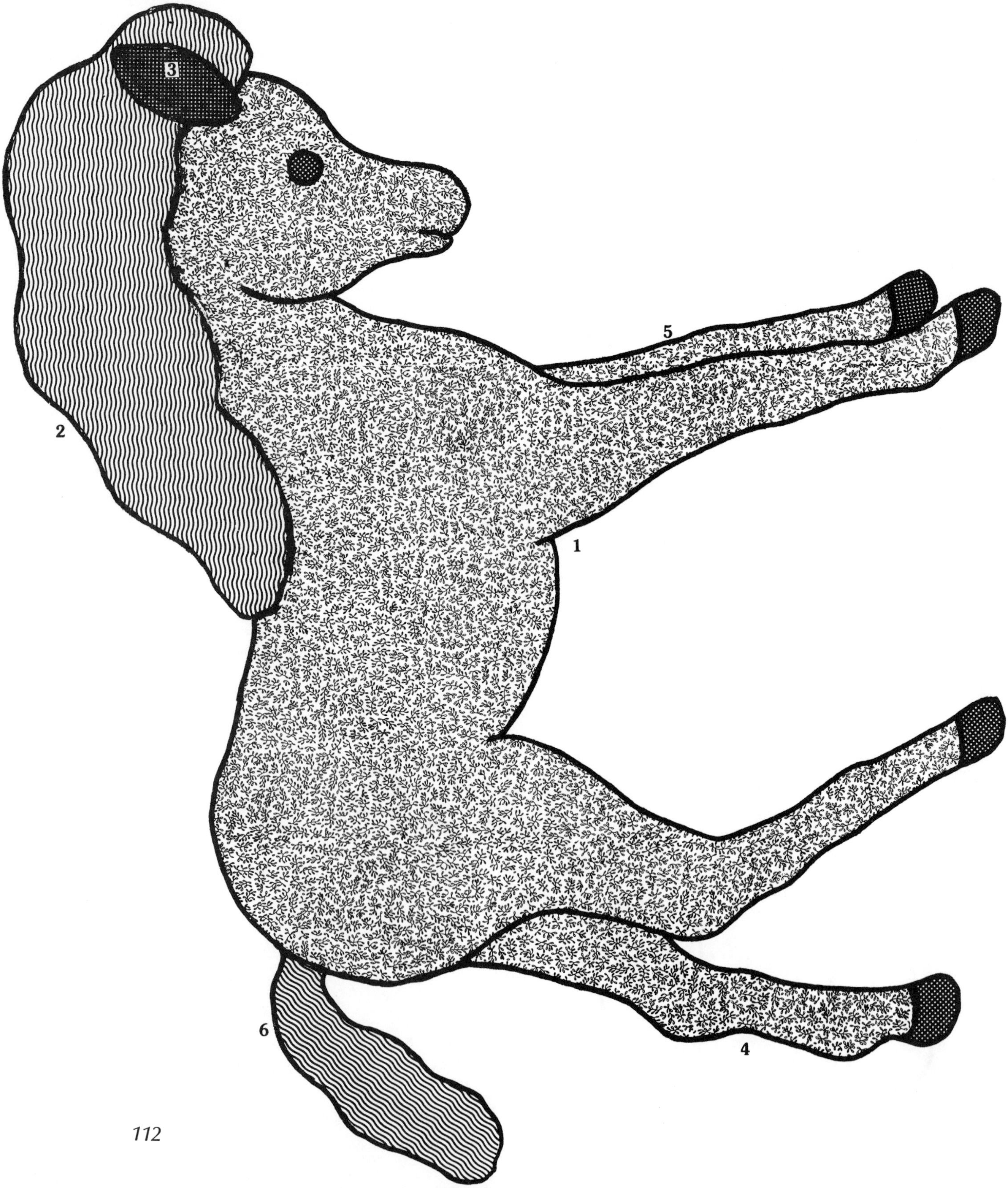

1

2

3

4

5

6

112

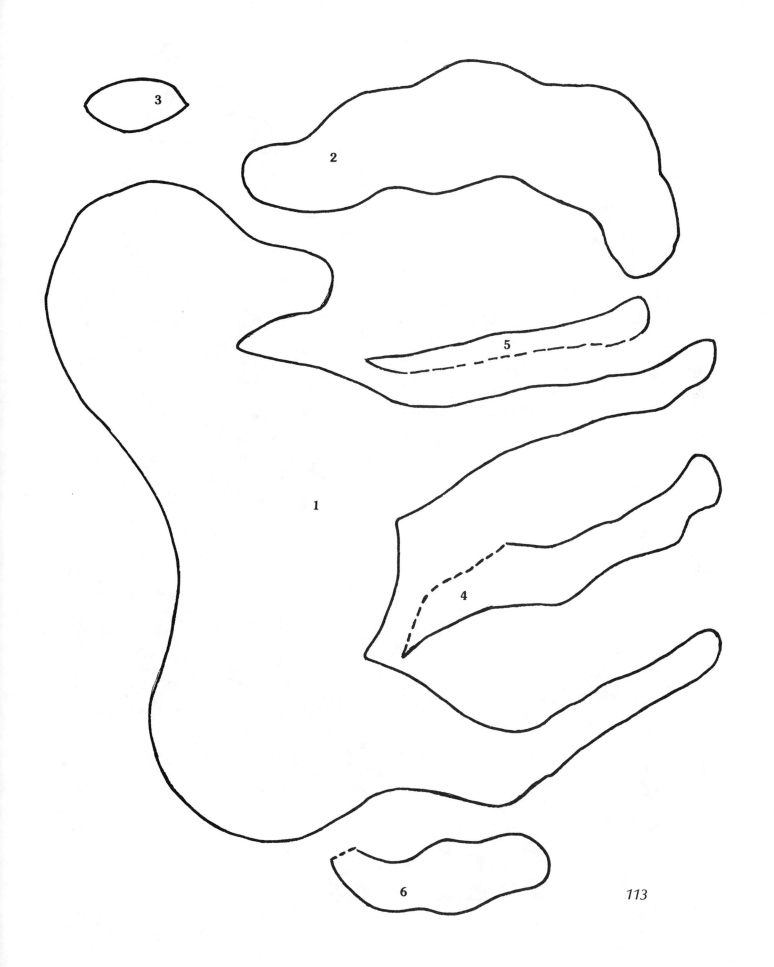

113

Clover Cow

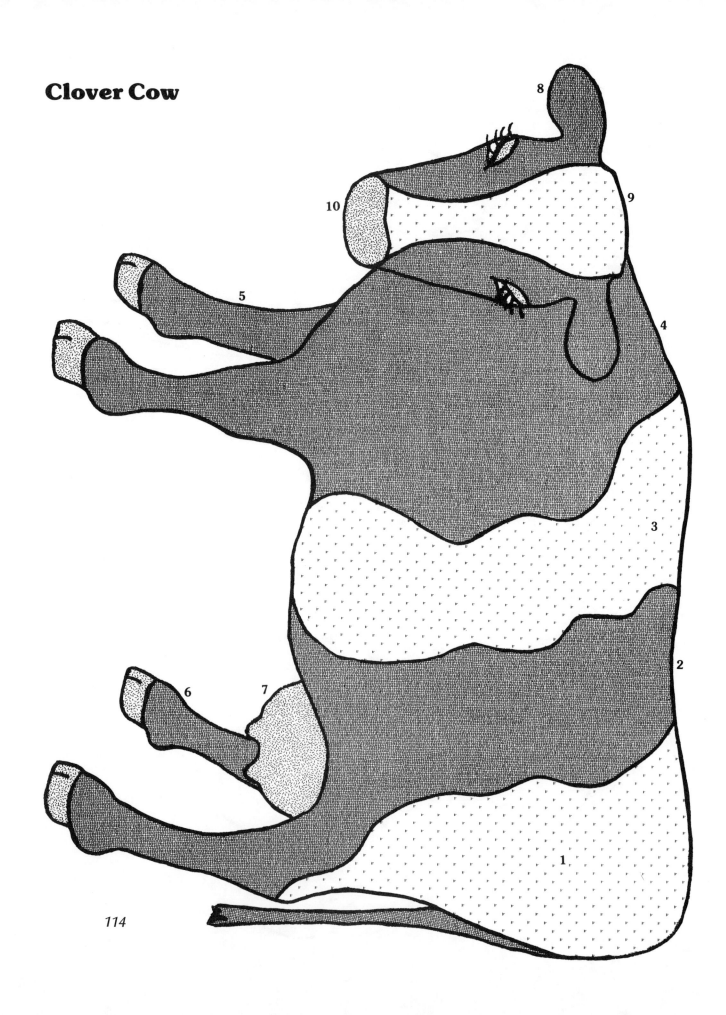

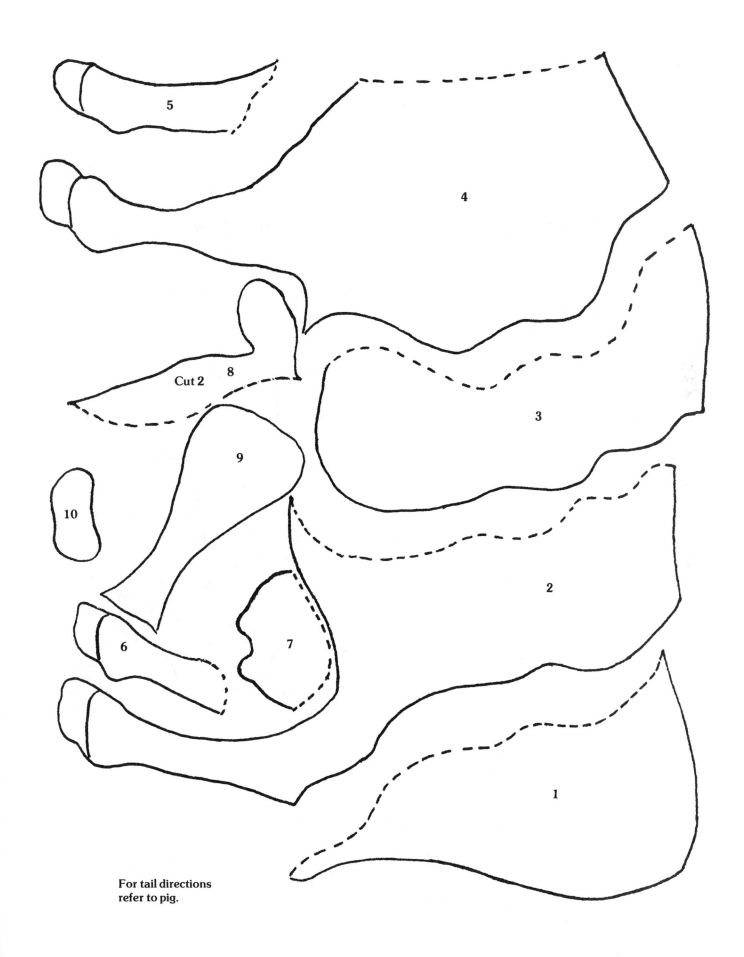

Cut 2

For tail directions
refer to pig.

Chuck Chicken

Chuch Chicken

Read and follow assembly directions for appliqué. Pieces 1–7 and 13 may be stuffed using the method given in assembly directions no. 6. Other pieces will be easier to handle if also cut in duplicate, stitched, and turned inside out. The broken lines indicate where seams are to be left open and overlapped. Use the numbered sequence for placement. Overlap where broken lines indicate. Slipstitch around pieces on the backing fabric.

Winky Owl

118

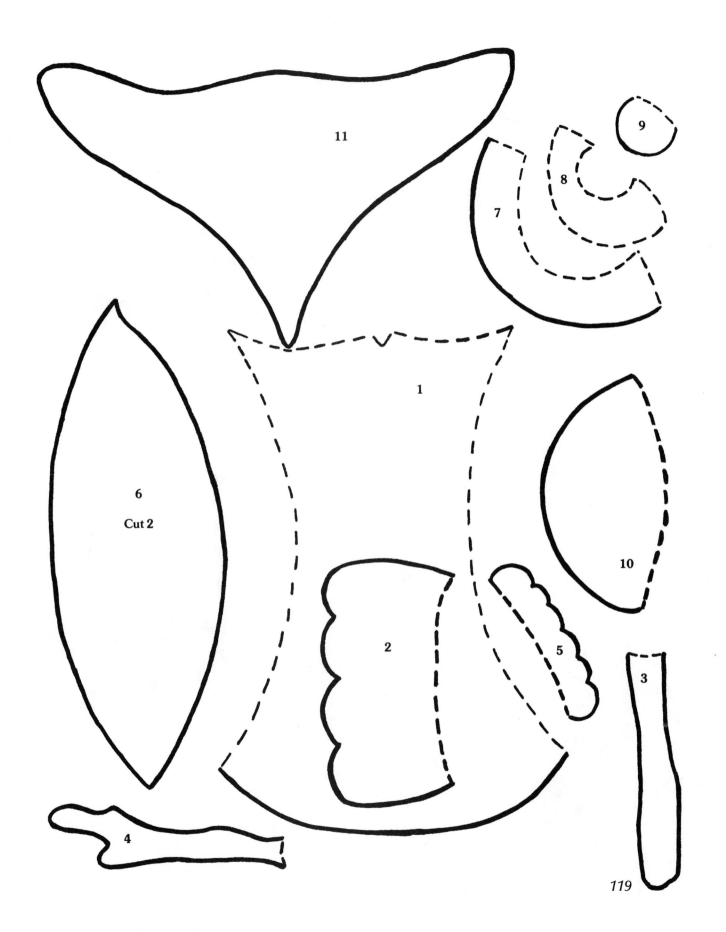

119

Daisy Sheep

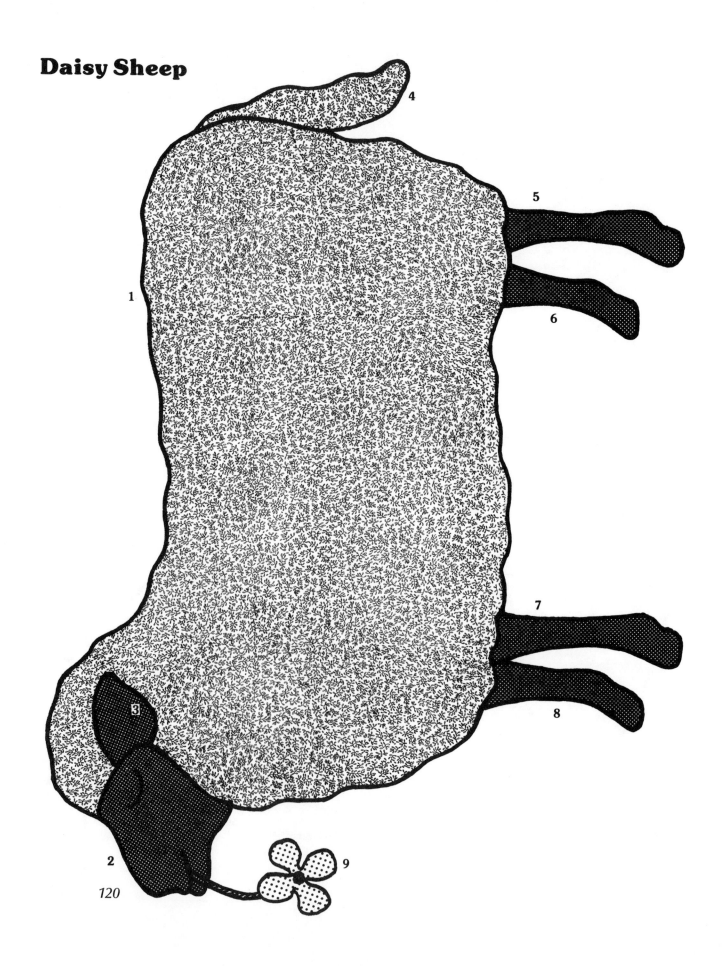

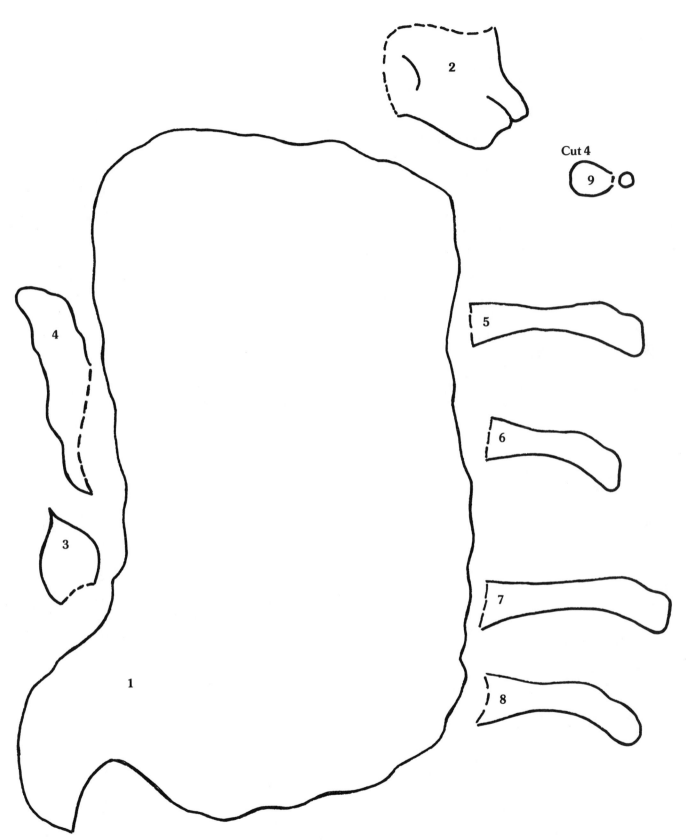

Cut 4

121

Sheep Wallhanging (18″ by 25″)

Materials

- Piece of fake fur for the sheep
- Strip quilting: fourteen strips of 1½″ by 7½″ fabrics
- Borders: two 2½″ by 14½″ and two 2½″ by 21½″ pieces of fabric
- Corners: four 2½″ squares of fabric
- Center backing piece for sheep: one 14½″ square of fabric
- Top hanging tabs: four 2½″ by 2½″ pieces

Directions

1. Cut the sheep from the fake fur and glue to the 14″ backing square. No seams are needed for the sheep.
2. Sew the fourteen strips together lengthwise. Add to the 14¼″ block with the sheep.
3. Add the side 2½″ by 21½″ borders.
4. Cut the corner squares and add to the 2½″ by 14½″ border strips. Stitch one strip to the bottom and the top of the wallhanging with right sides together. Press open. Baste the top, batting, and backing together and quilt. Bind the edges.

Make tabs for the top as follows: Fold the 2½″ strips in two, stitch, and reverse. Sew by hand or stitch in place.

Country sheep wallhanging with strip quilting

Trace each section and add seams. Follow appliqué directions.

A stylized cat to appliqué

125

Hawaiian Paper Cutting

Hawaiian paper cutting is similar to German Scherensnitte. It is a technique we probably have all been exposed to as children when we cut rows of dolls and soldiers from paper.

Directions (see figures)

1. Fold a square of paper in half.
2. Fold in quarters.
3. Fold again in eighths.
4. Shows completed eighths.
5. Folded paper ready to draw on.
6. Folds with design drawn.
7. Opened design.
8. Design reproduced from fabric and placed on a pillow backing.

Once a design is cut and placed on a backing, the traditional method is to turn under seam allowances on the design and hand quilt around it. Quilting designs are usually random and follow the shape of the design. They flow outward from the design like the waves that surround the islands of Hawaii.

An optional method is to back the design with iron on pellon leaving no seams to turn. Adhere the design to the backing fabric. Appliqué or blanket stitch around the design edge. Then proceed with hand quilting and a pillow finishing.

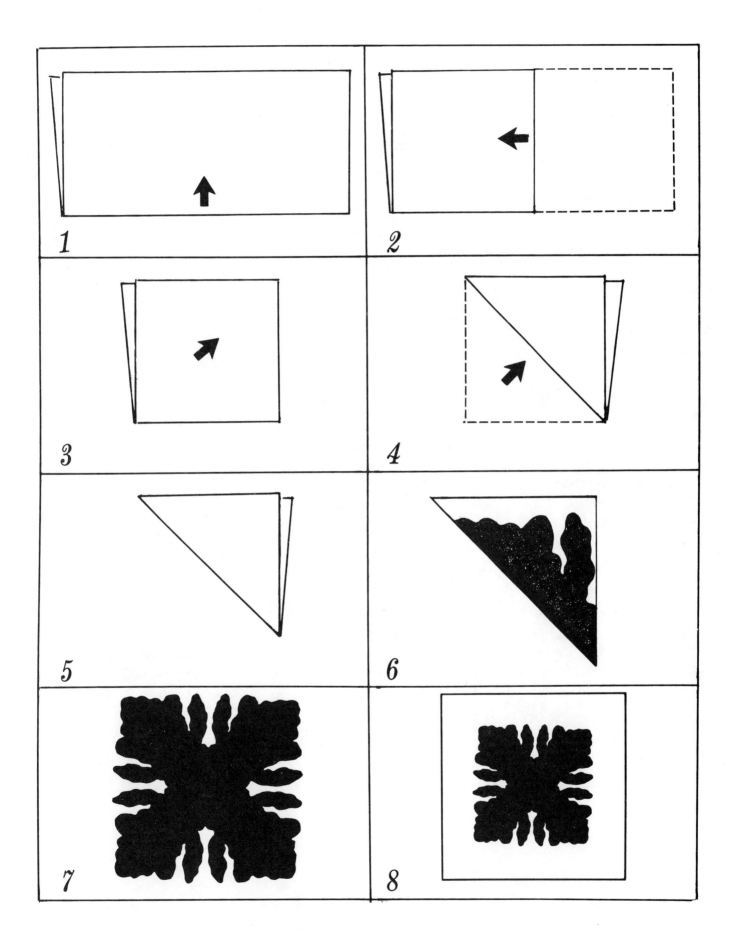

1

2

3

4

5

6

7

8

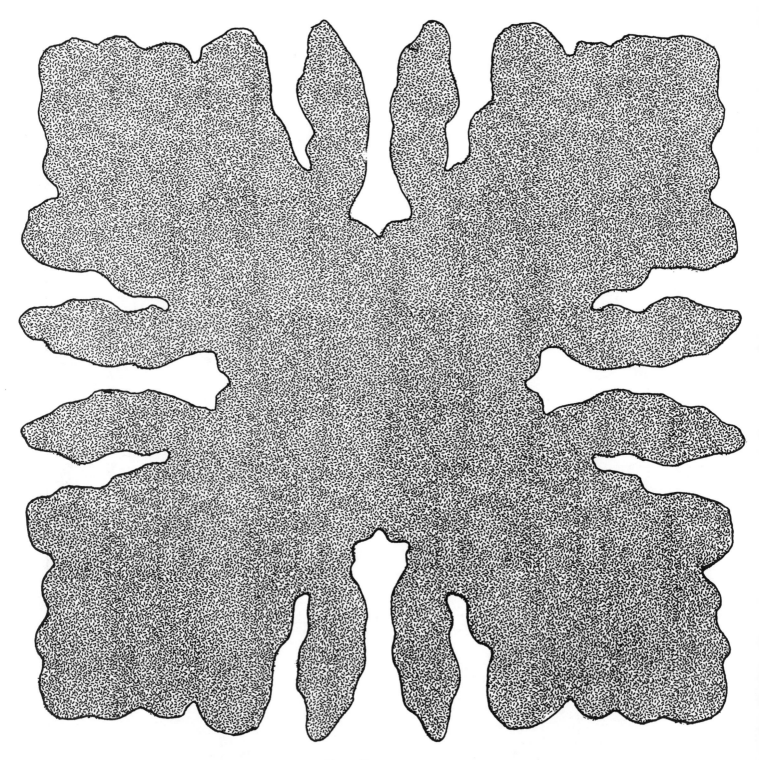

Hawaiian

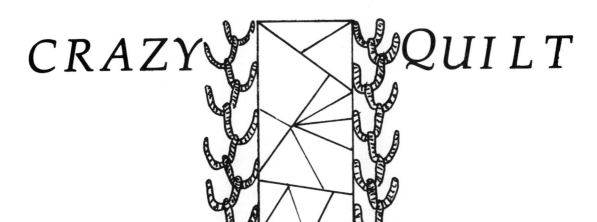

CRAZY QUILT

Chapter 9
Crazy Quilt
Memorabilia

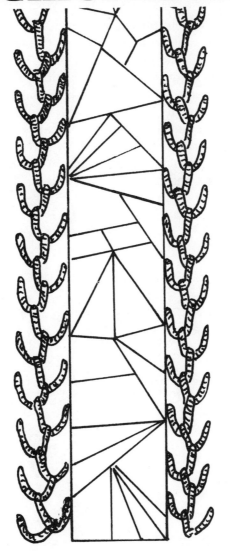

A legacy of the Victorian age is the random-shaped piecework of the crazy quilt. Assembled on backing fabric, the technique utilizes many elegant pieces of material. Enhancing the beauty of the textiles is the ornate stitchery that covers each seam. Crazy quilts differ from other quilts in that they do not have batting or hand quilting. Instead the top is tied to a backing piece of cloth with a center of flannel or wool. Originally the quilt was a decorative piece used as a throw in the Victorian parlor.

While visiting the Dwight D. Eisenhower home in Abilene, Kansas, I was delighted with a small crazy-quilt pillow sitting in a small sewing rocker in a parlor. The pillow, made by President Eisenhower's mother, included the embroidered names and birthdates of each of her sons. The sentiment of this charming piece is recalled in my own version of a family memory pillow. Unlike that earlier mother, we have a wide variety of fabrics to choose from. I selected crepe satin and lace. I drew random shapes which allowed space to embroider the names of my own children. In the center I embroidered my wedding date. Try this for a wedding, graduation, or birthday.

Crazy quilting also lends itself to enhancing clothing. Two vests are shown here. One consists of random shapes which allow for display of some choice crochet pieces on the front and back. The other was cut from old embroidered pillowcases which were arranged and embroidered together in the crazy-quilt fashion.

The first time I taught a class in crazy quilting, the students were reluctant to draw their own shapes. The technique should be spontaneous, and a pattern should not be necessary. However, at the time, I realized that some students would need direction, so I drew a pattern which is shown. The design is a suggested plan for making a pillow piece. Enlarge the square to a suitable size. Number each section so that you can assemble pieces after cutting.

First cut a backing square when making a crazy-quilt piece. Add pieces one at a time, turning edges under as they overlap. Seams are covered with embroidery stitches.

Crazy quilts were traditionally made of heavy, elegant fabrics such as velvets and were in solid colors. Contemporary crazy quilting is done with most fabrics available. However, stitchery shows best on a solid background of darker fabrics. If you like to embroider, crazy quilting is for you.

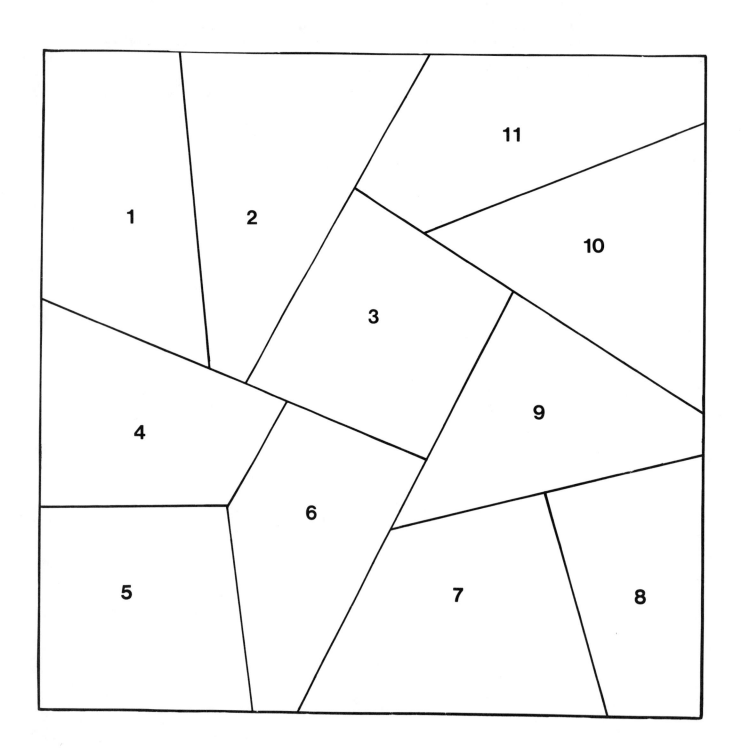

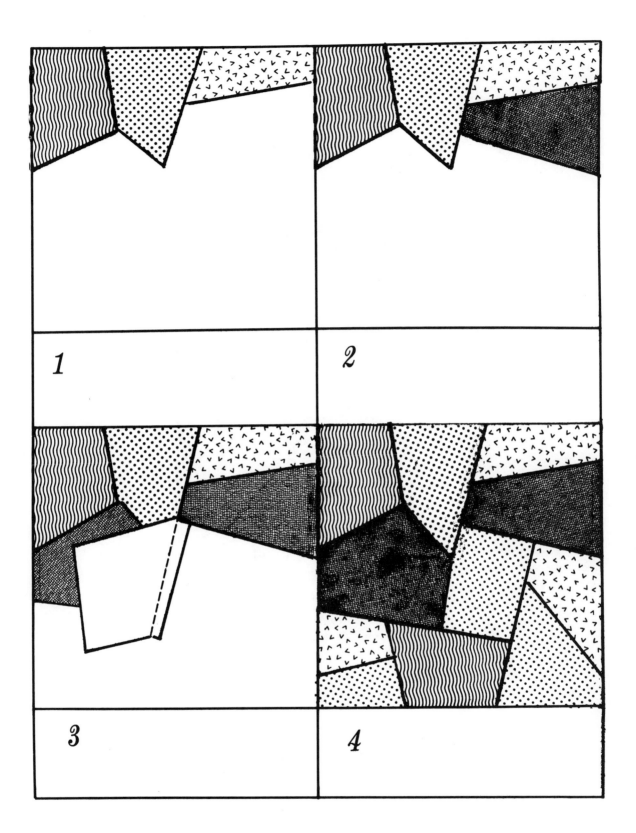

1

2

3

4

Crazy-quilt vests present an opportunity to utilize old crochet pieces. Decorate with choice buttons, pins, special fabrics, and other treasures.

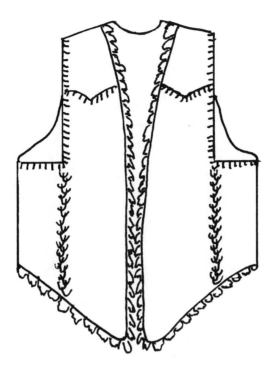
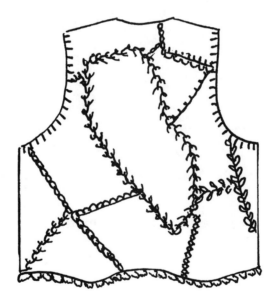

Old embroidered pillowcase vest. Pieces are cut up and sewn together. They are then embroidered. Even the old crochet edges are saved.

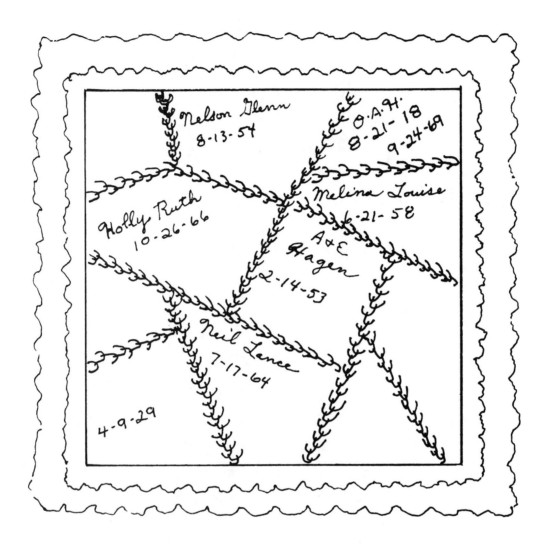

Mrs. Eisenhower's treasure becomes a modern inspiration. Embroider names, dates, and places.

Chapter 10
Heirloom Photo Dye Quilting

For a unique and treasured heirloom, try making a photo quilt. It can be assembled quickly but requires considerable planning. Mine took months to prepare and a day to sew together. The greatest time involves obtaining, selecting, and enlarging the photographs to be used. I found myself cajoling relatives to part with cherished pictures and begging brother William to please get his portrait taken so I would not have to use his baby picture. (I never got it.) There may be diplomatic decisions involving divorced relatives and second marriages. To settle possible misunderstandings, I made three quilts.

The method of reproduction that I used is photo dye printing. It is more expensive than the Cyanotype blueprint method done by hand, but I was reluctant to turn the bathroom into a chemical lab at this point. Since my house has become a quilter's haven, I did not care to press my luck with my husband any further.

The quilt size shown is for a double bed measuring 71" by 95". The quilt consists of thirty photographs in five rows horizontally and six rows vertically. Because the photographs used are 8" by 10", the individual blocks are a finished size of 9" by 11", a rectangular rather than a square block. The sashings between the pictures are 3" and the outer borders are 4". A low loft quilt batting and a sheet for the back were used.

Photo dye printing is done from positive, not negative, prints. Negatives are only needed to reduce or enlarge a picture. It is preferable to obtain good contrast photographs whether black and white or color. Along with family pictures, consider printing copies of wedding invitations, the family crest, awards, or other treasured documents. The first photo quilt I did was for my parents. I was able to obtain both their wedding announcement and that of my paternal grandparents. One block also includes a picture of a family reunion.

Photo dye printing is done on fabric with an approximate blend of 65 percent polyester and 35 percent cotton. Prewash fabrics first. Several colors of print are available: black, brown, red, green, royal, and navy blue. I prefer black on a gray fabric which gives the appearance of a continuous-tone photograph. A light fabric with blue ink gives a high contrast which loses some detail.

Before doing a large quilt, try a pillow first. Talk to your local T-shirt store about your plans. Make arrangements with the owner since doing thirty pictures at once involves additional time. Also discuss the option of having lettering printed at the same time. Either Roman or script should be available. Or plan to allow space to embroider your own details on the blocks. It is an opportunity to record some family history along with the photographs.

Should you decide to tackle the chemical method, it will require a very high-contrast Kodalith negative for each fabric printing. Also, the fabric should be all cotton and prewashed. The materials are highly toxic and must be stored carefully. Photo dye printing is an easier solution so consider it for your heirloom quilt.

Photo Quilt

Materials

For quilt blocks use 3 yards of polyester and cotton blend fabric (44″ wide fabric). Cut the blocks 10″ by 12″ for printing to be finished at 9½″ by 11½″ after printing. This gives some adjustment space should the pictures not be centered when printed. Allow some extra yardage in case the prints need to be redone.

For the sashing use 2½ yards. For borders use 2½ yards. For backing use one full-size sheet. For batting use low loft bonded 81″ by 96″.

Directions

1. Prewash fabrics.
2. Cut blocks for photos and get printing done. Trim to 9½″ by 11½″.
3. Cut twenty-five 3½″ by 9½″ strips for sashings.
4. Sew the vertical rows of blocks together with strips, making five rows of six pictures each.
5. Cut six 3½″ by 81½″ strips for vertical sashings between rows of blocks. With right sides together, pin and stitch the sashings between the blocks.
6. Cut and add 3¼″ by 63½″ sashings to the bottom and top of the quilt.
7. Cut and add 4½″ by 87½″ strips for borders to the sides of the quilt.
8. Cut and add 4½″ by 4½″ squares to a bottom and top border strip cut 4½″ by 63½″.
9. Mark all hand-quilting lines lightly on the quilt top. Baste the top, batting, and backing together well and proceed with quilting.

Photo Quilt

Cathedral Window Photo Dye Pillow

Materials

The pillow is made with four 16″ squares of calico.

- · 1 yard of calico
- · ¼ yard of border fabric
- · 2 yards of eyelet or lace
- · Pillow backing fabric ½ yard of calico
- · Photo blocks (squares) ¼ yard
- · Use cathedral window directions
- · Use pillow envelope directions

Assemble your pillow squares as directed. Trim your photo pictures to fit the triangular shape of the centers. Note that when you reproduce the photographs you must allow for the angled shape of the placement.

The pillow directions are the same as for cathedral window.

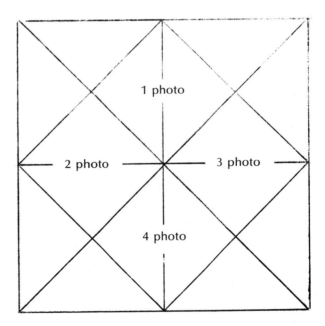

Photo Wallhanging

Materials

The wallhanging can vary in length as desired. Shown is a plan for five squares which gives four centers for portraits. It can be made of muslin, solids, or printed fabrics. The directions are the same as for the vest front piece.

Directions

1. Make five squares and attach them vertically by machine.
2. Before tacking the points together, stitch the piece along the flap folded lines to a backing piece. Add lace or trim if desired.
3. Turn the flaps to the center and tack by hand.
4. Place photo squares in the centers. Note that these centers are at an angle. This should be considered when printing and cutting.
5. Finish the turned edges, add a ring at the top, and hang.

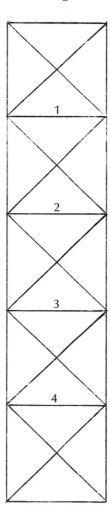

Other Photo Dye Projects

1. Photo your children's picture onto a skirt and have the words printed, "I LOVE MY CHILDREN."
2. If you have a child in an organization, print his or her picture on a shirt or apron with the name of the group. I did this on an apron when one of my sons was a De Molay boy. Now all of the mothers in the organization wear aprons to all fundraising breakfast and supper events with their sons' pictures and the words, "I LOVE DE MOLAY."
3. Greet your husband at home wearing a pinafore or apron that says, "I LOVE MY HUSBAND."
4. Say "HAPPY VALENTINE" with your pictures on a garment.
5. Put favorite photo pictures into a crazy-quilt piece.

Photo quilting has many possibilities and adds a very personal touch.

Chapter 11
Enhancing Garments

One of the many joys of quilting today is the practical application of designs to enhancing garments. Quilters have endless opportunities to express their creativity through apparel embellishment. Every quilt show now includes wearable art which is a testimony to the ingenuity of contemporary designers.

Among the techniques being used to embellish, I have suggested the following:

1. String and strip quilting
2. Quick patchwork methods
3. How to make a baldric
4. Dresden plate used on a jacket in two sizes
5. Dresden plate apron
6. Yo-yo as an embellishment
7. Puff or biscuit as a bag

Chapters 5 and 6 include suggestions for using the folded star and cathedral window as clothing embellishments.

Other techniques popular today are from past traditions and have been revived with enthusiasm. They include slashing and dagging. Slashing involves a grid plan of machine stitching with small diagonal slashes within each grid square. Dagging is also a cutting method but from the hem up into the skirt. Both techniques allow a display of multilayers of fabric by cutting. At one time a display of fabric layers was a sign of wealth.

Baldric

The idea of a baldric occurred to me when Queen Elizabeth visited California. Royalty was on everyone's mind, and the baldric has long been a symbol associated with royal dress. In the fifteenth century, the baldric was a decorative piece, a long silver band which ran diagonally from the right shoulder to the left hip and was edged in bells. The baldric shown here is pieced into a vest.

Directions

1. Select your favorite vest pattern.
2. Trace the pattern onto paper such as newsprint.
3. Draw the baldric lines as you would want them worn.
4. Cut out the width of the baldric from the paper.
5. Be sure to number all pieces before you assemble them.
6. Add seam allowances to each piece.
7. Cut fabric for each piece. Velour and super suede are shown.
8. Assemble the pieces and stitch.
9. Edge the baldric with braid.

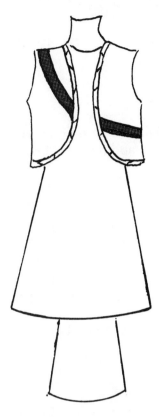

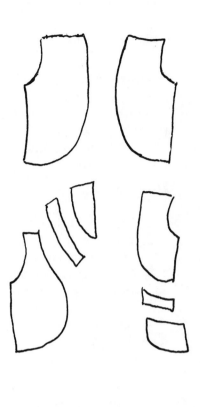

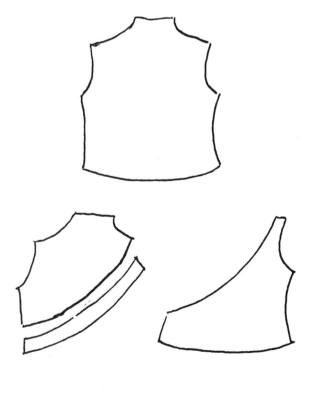

147

String Quilting

A simple string or strip quilting method can be used to cover yokes, bodices, pockets, or borders. It adds interest to a garment and makes each unique. Sometimes this technique can enhance a purchased garment by adding a pocket, belt, border, or vest.

Directions

1. Decide on the area to be covered and cut a backing piece of fabric.
2. Cut varied 1″ to 2″ strips of assorted fabrics.
3. Starting at one edge or corner, lay a strip flat.
4. With right sides together, stitch another strip along the edge of the previous strip. Open and press. Continue until the backing is covered. Trim edges.

Small patches can be assembled this way and placed on a garment. Finish edges with bias or braid.

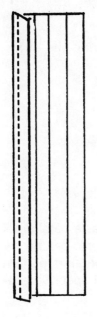

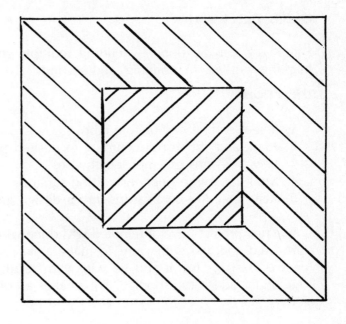

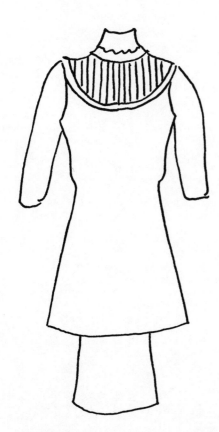

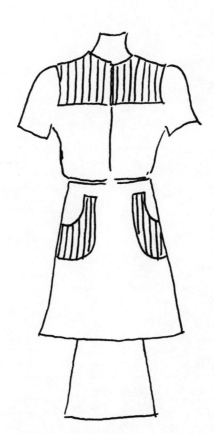

Quick Patchwork

Patchwork can be done by cutting multiple strips first, then sewing the strips, marking, cutting, rearranging, and sewing.

Directions

1. Select several compatible fabrics.
2. Mark and cut strips according to desired patch size. Include seams.
3. Sew the strips together lengthwise.
4. Mark crosswise lines for cutting squares.
5. Rearrange the patch strips into a design and stitch sides together.

The first project I ever attempted was done with this method. It was a patchwork skirt lined and tied with yarn. To make a skirt, first prepare the fabric patchwork for a skirt size. Line it and tie with yarn. Gather and finish as the skirt pattern suggests or add it to a bodice. This makes a colorful garment for a special occasion.

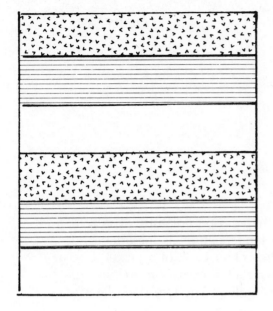

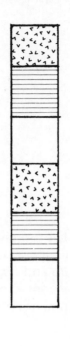

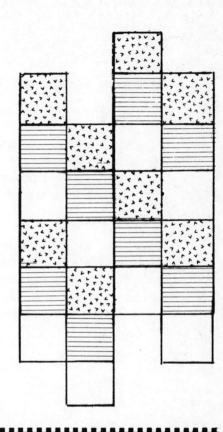

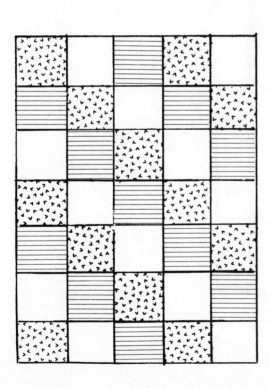

151

Dresden Plate Jacket

Materials

- Scraps of four materials
- Center of velour
- Favorite jacket pattern
- Bias made of velour

Directions

Directions for the Dresden plate are given in the chapter on miniatures. The center Dresden plate is from the miniature pattern. The larger pattern is included under sampler. Finish the entire plate and appliqué to the center back of a jacket. Use a second smaller plate on the front shoulder. The jacket shown is from pink pre-quilted material and edged in maroon velour bias binding. The Dresden plates are of calico.

An authentic Dresden plate pattern becomes the border for an apron and a center for a bib. Two sizes are given: a smaller version for the bib and a larger for the borders. Use your favorite pattern and add the appliquéd Dresden plates.

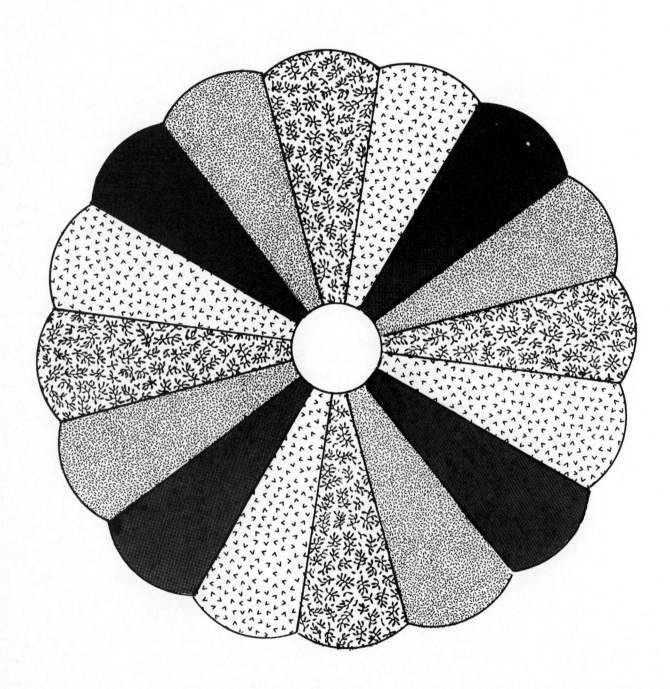

Yo-yo

This pattern has been popular in modern quilt history as a way of utilizing scraps. The small gathered circles are sewn together to make a colorful quilt top. Another use is to string the circles into various shapes. Yo-yos make attractive decorations for clothing and can be sewn into a vest. The yo-yo finished size is half of the original circle pattern.

Directions

1. Make a template 3½" in diameter.
2. Make another template 3" in diameter.
3. Make a paper template 1½" in diameter.
4. Trace the largest circle on the wrong side of fabric.
5. Baste around the circumference of the fabric circles.
6. Place the medium-sized circle (3") on the wrong side of the fabric circle center. Pull the basting thread to form a ¼" seam. Press over the template. Then remove the template.
7. Baste the seamed edge. Put the small paper circle in the center and pull the second basting thread tight to form a circle the paper size. Slip the paper out and secure the gathered edge in place.
8. Join the circles together at the edge.

To decorate a garment, join a string of yo-yos and appliqué to a skirt or vest.

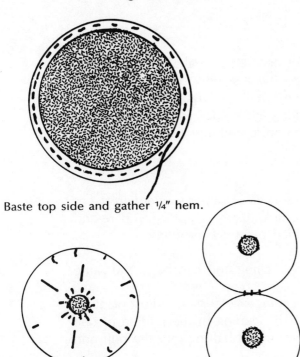

Baste top side and gather ¼" hem.

Baste top side and gather yo-yo.

Use yo-yos on a skirt and vest.

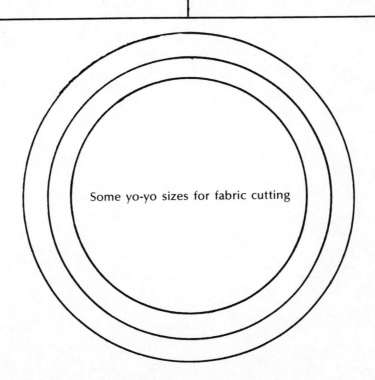

Some yo-yo sizes for fabric cutting

Puff Quilting

The puff or biscuit is a fun technique which can be used to make a quilt, pillow, handbag, or even a vest or coat. It is formed by the assembly of two squares of unequal size. Sizes of the puffs can vary from small to large. There are also variations on the methods of gathering and forming the shapes. Puffs can be filled with batting before they are closed and do not require quilting. Assembly is done on the sewing machine.

Directions

Suggested fabrics for puffs: gingham, prints, solids, velour, super suede, velveteen, satin, most any fabric which is not bulky. For a pillow, use a 3″ bottom square and a 4½″ top square. The pillow has eight ⅝″ folded pleats at the corners.

1. Cut two sizes of squares. The bottom is a backing and can be of the same material or something lighter in weight.
2. Pin the two cut pieces together with wrong sides together and adjust pleats at the corners. Baste the edges, leaving a small opening in the middle of one side for stuffing. Put batting or a square of bonded batting into the puff and stitch the hole.
3. Assemble rows of puffs with right sides together and stitch a ¼″ seam.
4. For a 12″ square pillow, use twenty-five puffs. Cut twenty-five 3″ bottoms and twenty-five 4½″ tops. Assemble five puffs to a row.

This same method can be used to make a bag, a vest, or a coat. Assemble the project and line.

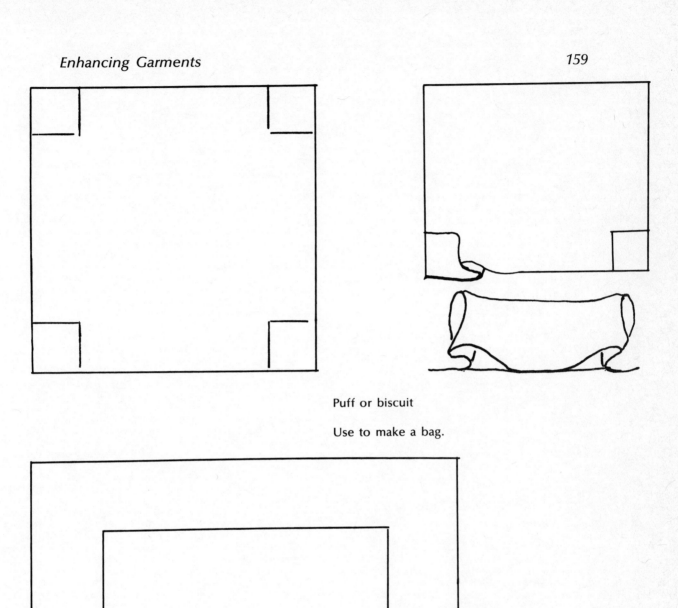

Puff or biscuit

Use to make a bag.

Chapter 12
Old Traditions:
Stencil, Candlewick,
and Twill

Stencil: A Colonial Art Form Revived

Stencil work consists of filling in an open area of design with fabric paints. For a solid application on fabric, a circular motion is used to burnish the area. Fabric stenciling requires a thicker paint than a hard surface. A variety of stencil paints is now available at quilt shops and shows.

Stencils are available ready-made or they can be cut. To design a stencil an X-acto knife, an electric pen, or a stencil knife is used. Materials to make stencils vary from mylar sheets to improvising with plastic covers or even freezer paper.

For a first attempt at stencil work, cut a design from freezer paper. Tape the paper over a design and cut the design out. Save the small pieces from the design. Bits and pieces can be used in this method. Next, position the paper design on the fabric with small pieces in the open area. With a medium-hot iron, press the design parts tight so that paint will not get through. With a circular motion, burnish the area to be covered. Peel the stencil off and use again. Dry with a hair dryer if you are in a hurry.

Other materials needed to stencil include a clear ruler, design pen, masking tape, stencil burnisher brush, stencil paints, and cutting tools. Small scissors may do if you use freezer paper. Try each method and find what suits you best.

Country Stenciled Pinafore

The pinafore is designed around commercial printed fabric squares which have a stenciled look. Cut nine 6½″ squares to start. Complete the sides with 1½″ strips attached in the log-cabin method. First add a strip across the top of the 6½″ block, matching right sides together. Stitch and press open. Repeat this method clockwise on the right, bottom, and left sides until two strips are added to each side, top, and bottom. This makes a 10½″ block from which to make a border strip. Add the blocks together to add to a skirt, apron, or pinafore. Finish the top and bottom borders with eyelet, braid, or ruffle. Use the same method to make a block to form a bodice front. Incorporate this into a favorite commercial apron pattern.

Country Baby Stenciled Quilt (25½″ by 35½″)

Make the six animal stenciled blocks from the patterns shown. Center each animal in a hex sign circle. These are typical of the Pennsylvania Dutch signs. To achieve a clean design on the fabric, center a circle of freezer paper and iron it in place. Make a plastic or paper stencil for the scalloped border. Position and paint. Remove the center paper. Position the animal stencil and paint each carefully. Finish the printed squares with the log-cabin method given for the pinafore above. Combine the squares into two rows of three each. Combine the rows. Add a 1″ and a 2″ border to the edges. Add batting and backing and quilt. Bind to finish.

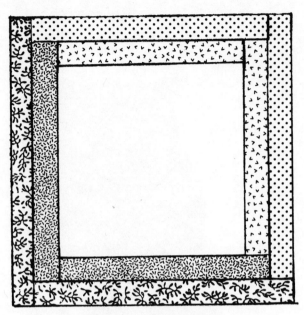

Log cabin border

Stencils on garments

Center designs within this typical hex sign border.

Candlewicking

Materials

- No. 2 crewel embroidery needle or no. 20 chenille needle
- Belding Lily 20/3 cotton thread or six-strand embroidery floss
- Candlewicking thread is also available
- Marking pencil
- Household paraffin optional
- 100 percent cotton fabric (do not prewash)
- Hoop

Directions

1. Mark or trace dots of a design onto your fabric.
2. Place in a hoop and tighten.
3. Select a thread and color. Vary thread weights for a different look.
4. Add embroidered embellishments for interest. Add small yo-yo circles for flowers. Try some twilling stitches to outline areas.

Candlewick Knot

1. Bring the needle up at the first dot shown.
2. Make a figure eight.
3. Place your needle against the fabric and under the thread, pulling the thread to the left with your left hand. Wind the thread once in a figure eight across the needle and over the tip of the needle. Insert the needle back into the fabric close to where you came out and pull.
4. Come up at the next dot and repeat.
5. Wash the finish piece to tighten the knots.

WELCOME

Twilling

Another colonial art is twilling, which consists of knots connected to each other giving a continuous outline to designs. Like candlewicking, twilling is fast and simple. You probably already know how to do the stitch since twilling has been called by other names over the years, such as double knot.

Materials

- A no. 2 sharp needle
- Hoop
- 1 strand of article 89 DMC cotton thread
- Kettle cloth or equivalent closely woven polyester fabric

Directions

Twilling is worked from top to bottom. To start, mark a line with a pencil. Bring the needle up through point A. Cross diagonally to one side, insert the needle at B, and come up at C. Now, without piercing the fabric, pass the needle under the thread at the first point A. With the thread under the needle, again pass through the lower part of the stitch. This completes the first knot. Continue a space below the same way, making a chain of knots. Pull loosely.

Use twilling to decorate clothing, padded picture frames, bags, and curtains.

Twill on straight lines and candlewick on dots.

Twilling Knot

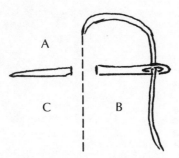

Knot your thread and come up at A. Pull gently and insert the needle at B and come up at C. Work back and forth across an imaginary line as indicated.

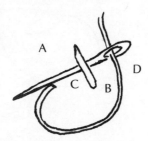

Pull from C and insert the needle again under the thread from right to left without piercing the fabric.

Repeat, inserting the needle below the previous thread. Now start another stitch below.

Double French Knot

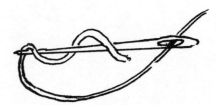

Come up at dot, twist the needle twice around the thread in the same spot, insert the needle into the fabric at about the same spot, and pull.

Colonial Knot
Bring the needle up at the dot.

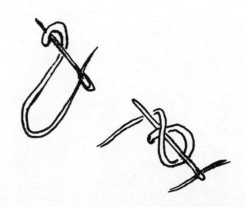

TOOTH FAIRY

Each of these 8" pillows has a small ½" pocket for a tooth. To make the small pocket, cut 1" by ¾" fabric piece. Turn under ¼" seams on three sides. Turn under ¼" and another ¼" on top. Stitch seam at top by hand. Stitch to backing. Embroider "Tooth Fairy" and name of child. Add flowers and borders. Finish pillow.

TOOTH FAIRY

Chapter 13
Quick Gifts

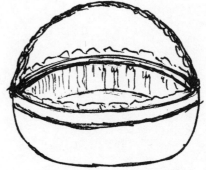

Crazy Quilt Christmas Ornament

Materials

· Scraps of fabrics
· Embroidery needle
· Thread

Directions

1. With fabric doubled, cut two lining pieces from the stocking pattern shown.
2. Cut two plain stocking pattern pieces for the crazy-quilt backing. Using scraps, crazy quilt the backing pieces. Embroider around the edges.
3. With right sides together, stitch the lining pieces together. Do not turn.
4. With right sides together, stitch the crazy-quilted stocking pieces together. Turn and press.
5. Place the lining inside the finished stocking. Finish the top with bias or a hem.
6. Make a loop to hang.

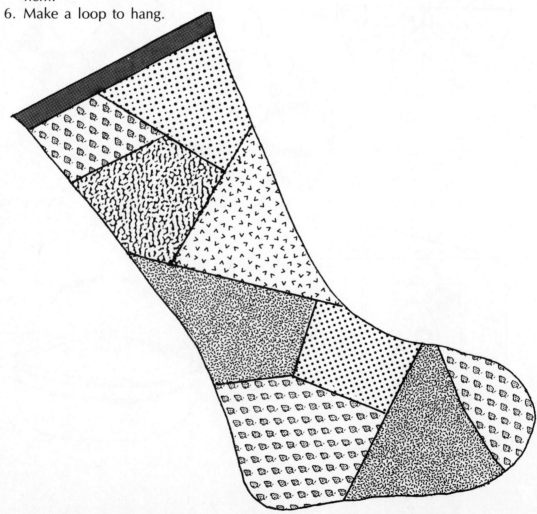

Patchwork Ornaments

Materials

· Styrofoam balls (3" suggested)
· Scraps of fabric
· Ribbon and glue

Directions

1. For ball 1, glue and press random fabric shapes into the foam with a corner poker.
2. Continue until the ball is covered and edges are not showing.
3. Pin a ribbon at the top for hanging.
4. For ball no. 2, cut eight almond-shaped fabric pieces from scraps.
5. Glue and press in place, overlapping slightly to fit.
6. Glue ribbon over the raw edges. Decorate with beads.
7. Make a loop to hang.

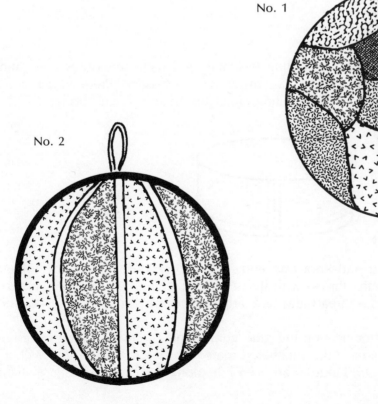

No. 1

No. 2

Glue Gun Basket Linings

Materials

- *Fabric length:* Measure around the top inner circumference and double the measurement.

- *Fabric width:* Measure from the top inside rim to the bottom and add 4" to 5".
- *Fabric for bottom:* Measure bottom of basket and add 2" to 3".
- *6 oz. batting & matboard:* Make a paper pattern of bottom. Cut batting and matboard to fit.
- *Crochet thread:* Measure inside top rim circumference and add 1". Glue gun and glue sticks available at hardware stores. Trimmings of ribbon, rick rack, and flowers optional.

Directions

1. Prepare a tube of fabric according to length and width measurements, and sew lengths together with ¼" seams where necessary. Press under a 2" allowance on top edge. Baste a line along the bottom for gathering.

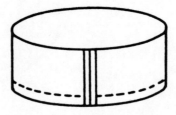

2. Cut crochet thread and knot one end. Stitch to secure 1" from the folded edge. Zigzag over the thread with the sewing machine, gathering as you go. At the end, knot the thread and tack adjacent to the other knot. Adjust the gathers.
3. Follow directions for heating the glue gun, being careful to place covering underneath work area. Adjust gathered material along the basket top with 1" extending above. Drop glue in an even line along the gathered edge a small

area at a time. Press as you go. Keep glue off your hands! Gather up bottom raw edges to fit basket, and drip glue in places to hold.

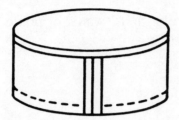 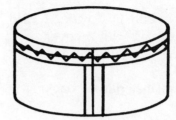

4. Prepare bottom piece from paper pattern. Glue batting to matboard shape. Gather fabric edge over padded board and pull tight, gluing in place as you press. Glue to the bottom over raw edges.
5. Trim as desired. Try lining a trunk.

Ribbon Folded Stars on a Basket

Materials

- Floral ribbon 1¼" wide, 1 yard of solid color and 2 yards of printed
- Small basket with a cover
- Hot glue gun or other glue
- Lace
- Scrap of material for backing the star

Directions

1. Cut the ribbon into 2½" lengths with sixteen of a print and twelve of a solid color. Extra ribbon will trim the basket bottom.
2. Fold the ribbon pieces into pie-shaped triangles by folding the top corners wrong sides together to the bottom center. Line up the pie shapes on a marked backing piece as for the folded star. Place four at the center and then make three rows of eight each. Glue each tip.

The ribbon gives a dimensional look as it lies stiff one layer upon the other. Add ribbon and lace to trim the basket bottom.

Quick Potholder Design

Cut two 7½" squares from a light fabric.
Cut two 7½" squares from a dark fabric.
Cut one 7" square of cotton batting.
Assemble the squares together one on top of the other as follows:

1. A dark fabric wrong side up
2. A light fabric wrong side up
3. The batting square
4. A dark fabric right side up
5. A light fabric right side up

Baste all layers together around the edges and diagonally.
Trace the design shown on a piece of paper and pin it to the layers.
Use your machine and do a zigzag stitch in satin stitch across each line of the paper design. Peel the paper off. With embroidery scissors, carefully cut through one layer of fabric to the stitched edges in marked areas. Repeat on the other side. This will leave a reverse pattern in the areas cut. Each side will also be in reverse if directions are followed.
Bind the project.

Quick Potholder

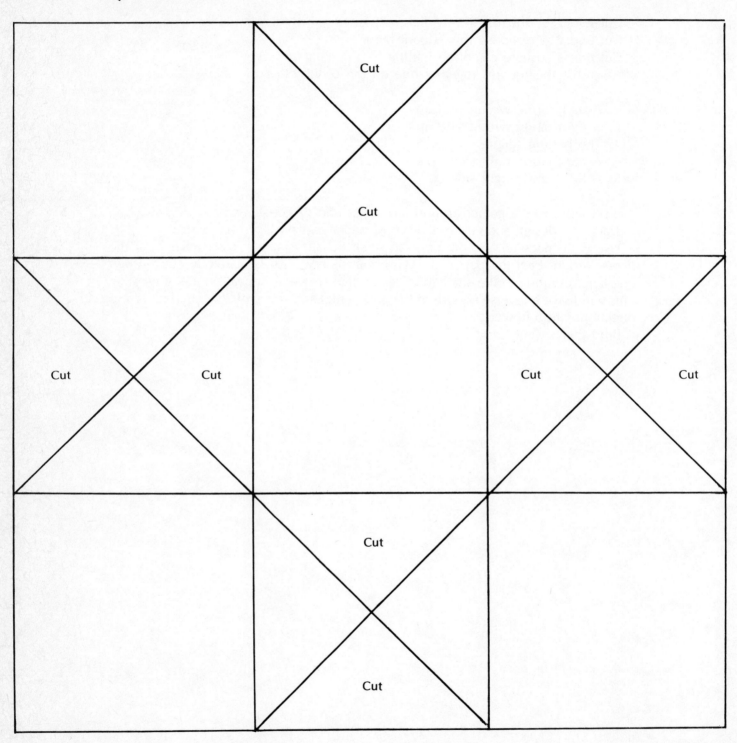

Christmas Folded Star Foam Ball

Materials

- A 3" styrofoam ball
- About ⅛ yard of coordinated dark and light prints and plain fabrics
- Ribbon or braid
- Floral pins
- Two pearl corsage pins
- Thread

Directions

With the thread, mark the circumference of the ball in half and pin.

Again with thread, mark quarters and eighths. These are guidelines for pinning the star pieces in place.

Cut 2" squares as follows:

- 8 of center color fabric A
- 16 of fabric B
- 16 of fabric C
- 16 of fabric D

Sew tips of four folded star pieces together for the center. Repeat for the bottom center. Secure the tips in place with a floral pin underneath the folded point. Place your corsage pin at the center. Adjust the rows of stars, eight points to a row, around the ball with a space of ½" between tips. Lift each star point and pin in place. Make three rows from each center, ending with raw edges at the ball middle.

Follow the thread guidelines for placement. Pin, adjust, and glue.

Cover the unfinished edges with ribbon and glue. Put on a loop for hanging.

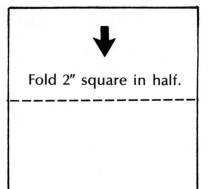

Fold 2″ square in half.

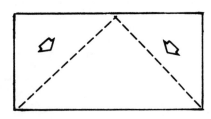

Make a pie shape.

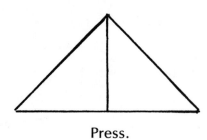

Press.

Mark ball circumference in eighths.

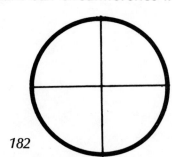

182

Folded Star Christmas Ball

Stitch four pieces for center and pin.

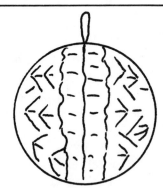

Continue until the ball is covered
and finish edges with ribbon.

Ball with four rows on each side

Dimensional Ball

Materials

- One 12-ounce bag of stuffing
- ¼ yard of two fabrics

Directions

There are two pattern pieces. The ball consists of twelve stuffed triads. Each triad is assembled with one of pattern number 1 and two of pattern number 2.

1. Cut twelve pieces from pattern no. 1.
2. Cut twenty-four from pattern no. 2.
3. With right sides together, match the curved sides of patterns 1 and 2 and sew together from A to B on both sides. Clip the curves. With right sides together, sew sides C and D, leaving a small hole to stuff. Continue assembling all twelve triads. Turn them inside out. Stuff and sew closed.
4. Combine three triads together at points 1, 2, and 3.
5. Continue until all four sections with three triads are assembled.
6. Combine the four sections by sewing together at the tips.

The selection of a dark and a light fabric will add to the dimensional appearance of the ball. For an additional project, a smaller pattern is given for a mobile.

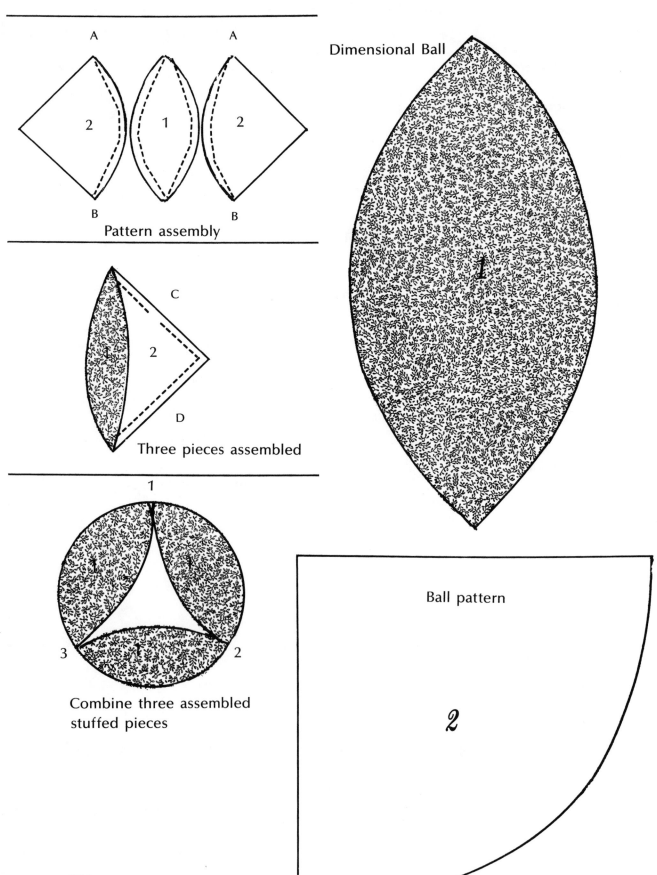

A

A

2

1

2

B

B

Pattern assembly

C

2

D

Three pieces assembled

1

3

2

Combine three assembled
stuffed pieces

Dimensional Ball

1

Ball pattern

2

184

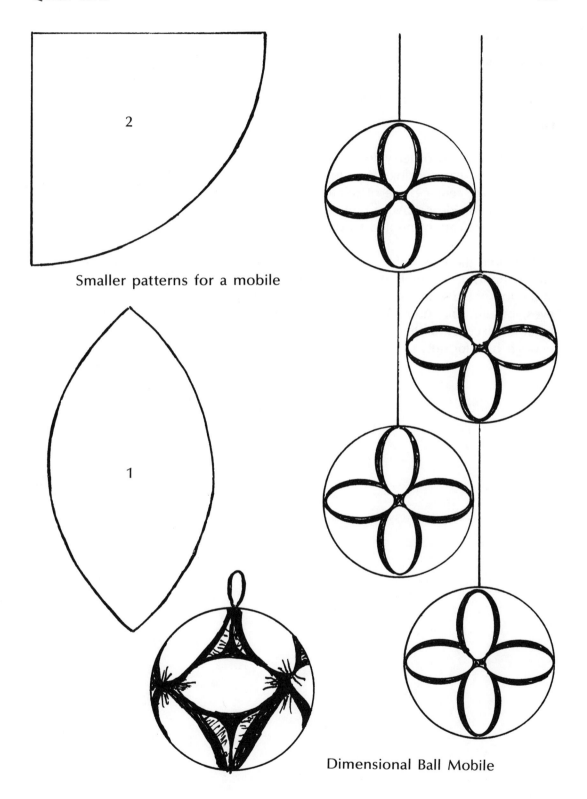

Smaller patterns for a mobile

Dimensional Ball Mobile

Floppy Ears Baby Bib

Materials

Two prints, terrycloth, and flannel for lining optional

Directions

1. With a piece of terrycloth folded, cut the pattern piece A.
2. Cut two ear backings from terrycloth.
3. Cut one center piece of printed fabric from B.
4. Cut two side pieces of printed fabric from C.
5. Cut two ears of printed fabric.

Assemble the ears right sides together from the printed and terrycloth fabrics. Stitch and turn. Assemble pieces B and C along the curve, adding the finished ears at the top of the seam. Stitch, trim the seam, and press the seam up. Embroider the eyes, mouth, and nose. With right sides together, stitch the front and backing together except for the neck. Turn and press. Bind the neck with bias, adding enough bias for ties. Use the ears to wipe the dribbles.

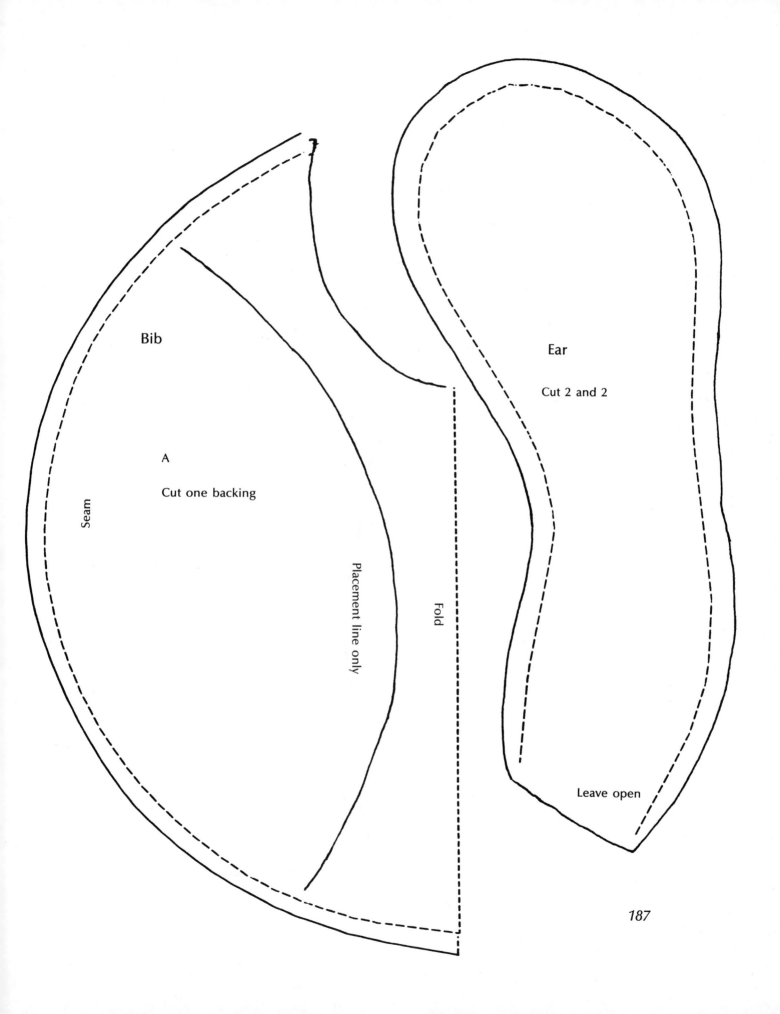

Bib

Ear

A

Cut 2 and 2

Cut one backing

Seam

Placement line only

Fold

Leave open

187

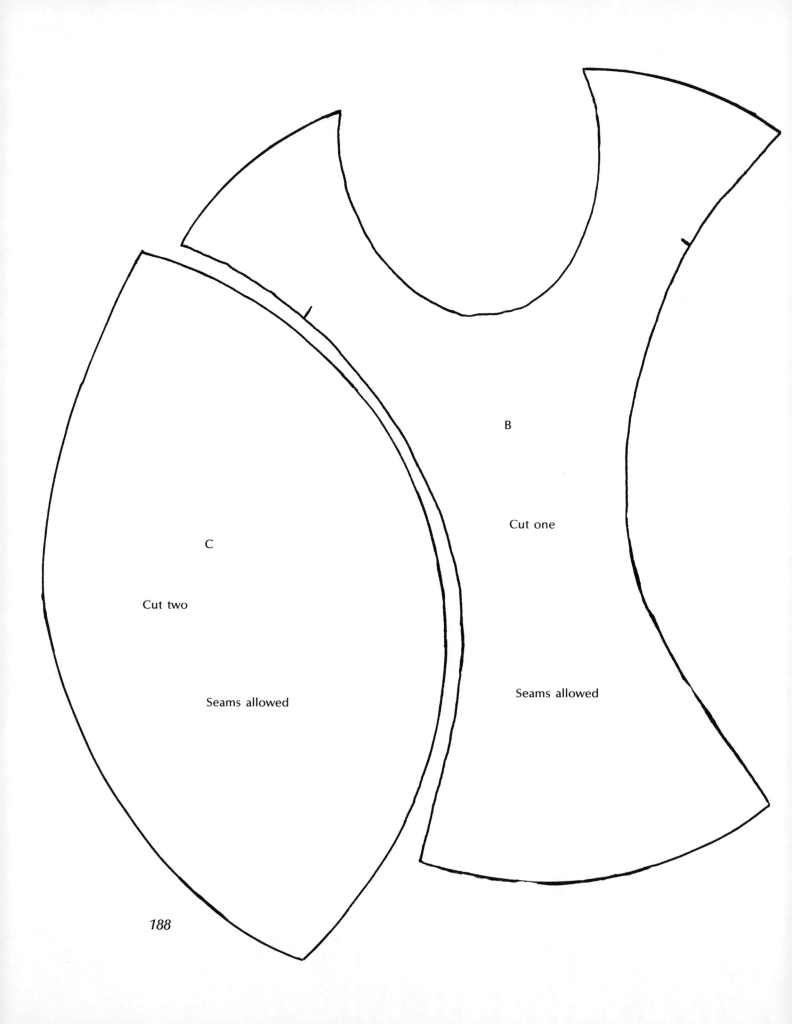

B

Cut one

Seams allowed

C

Cut two

Seams allowed

188

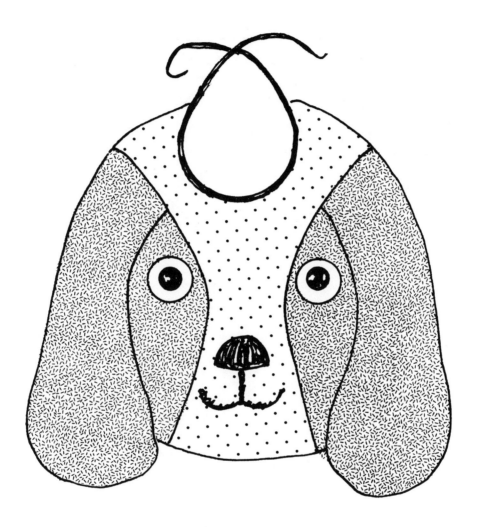

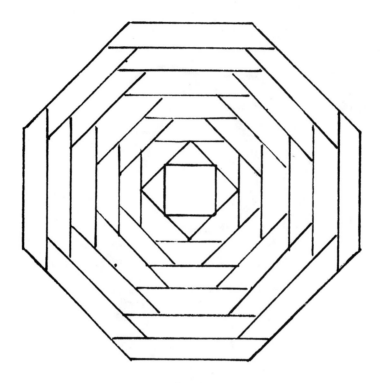

Pineapple Log Cabin Placemat
(Follow pattern for pillow, leaving corner pieces out.)

Log Cabin Pineapple Pillow

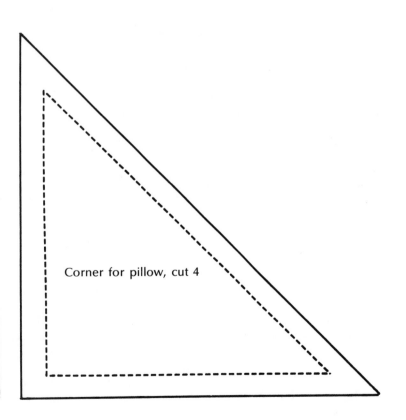

Center piece, cut 1

Corner for pillow, cut 4

191

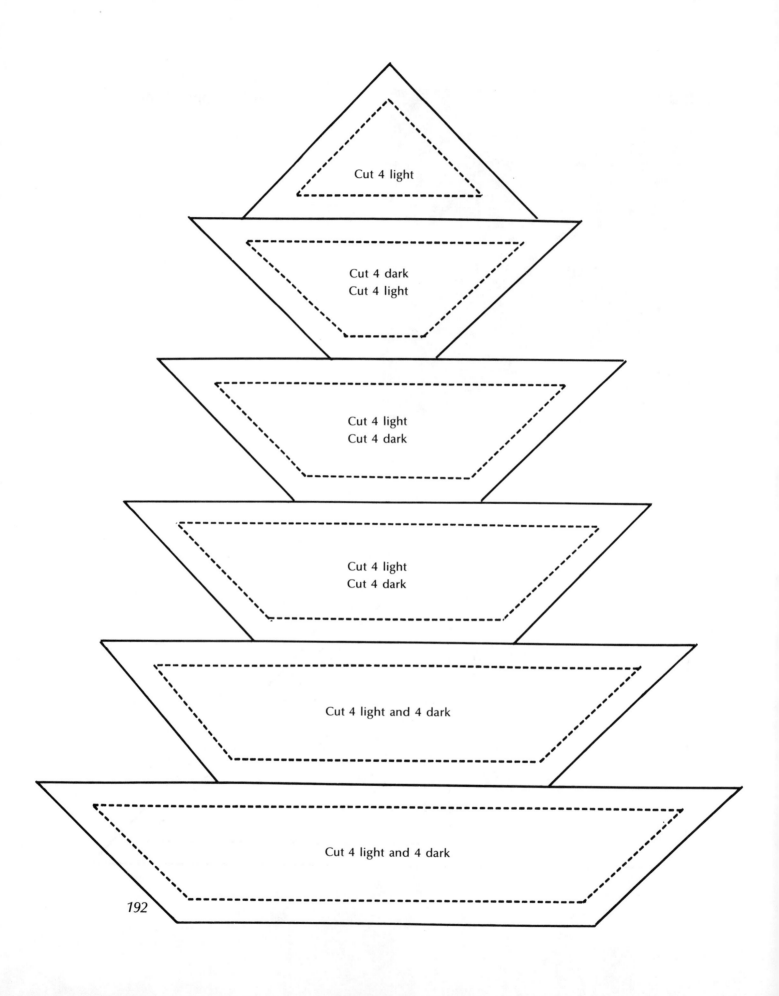

Cut 4 light

Cut 4 dark
Cut 4 light

Cut 4 light
Cut 4 dark

Cut 4 light
Cut 4 dark

Cut 4 light and 4 dark

Cut 4 light and 4 dark

192

1. Mark guidelines on a backing piece of muslin.
2. Center square in place.
3. Add triangles to each side, matching seam lines carefully. Press open.
4. Continue adding smallest to largest pieces clockwise around, matching seams each time. Press.
5. For a pillow, finish with binding. For a placemat, leave the corners off.

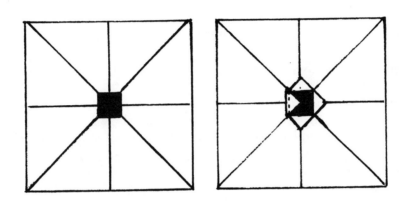

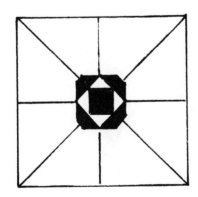

Fabric Wreath

Materials

- One 10″ styrofoam beveled wreath
- 1 yard of selected fabric, print, eyelet, gingham, etc.
- 90″ of gathered lace
- Ribbon for bow or fabric

Directions

1. Cut 1 yard of 45″ wide fabric in half crosswise, making two 18″ by 45″ pieces.
2. With right sides together, seam the ends of the two pieces together, making a continuous 90″ by 18″ piece.
3. Press one 90″ length of fabric, making a 4½″ hem with wrong sides together.
4. On the opposite side, press under ½″ hem and then a 4½″ hem.
5. Insert the lace under the finished edge of fabric edge, overlapping the opposite raw edge. Stitch the length of fabric, making two tubes.
6. Cut a 2″ section of styrofoam from the wreath. Feed one end of the tube on with lace projecting out. Glue the 2″ section back and hold with T pins until dry.
7. Add a bow, berries, flowers.

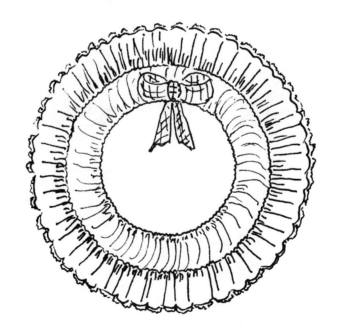

Album Cover with Photo

Materials

- 1 large photo album
- 1 yard of taffeta fabric
- ½ yard of batting
- Cardboard for photo frame
- Glue and a sharp knife
- Ribbon, lace, or flowers for trim

Directions

Album covering
Allow 1 yard of material.

1. Open the album and lay flat on a piece of paper. Trace a pattern piece and allow a 1" seam all around. Cut fabric.
2. Cut two inner cover pieces with seam allowances the same way, tracing a pattern to cover the inside from outside edges to the center rings.
3. Cut batting to fit the album pieces without seam allowances.
4. Lay the open fabric pieces with the wrong sides up and glue batting pieces to the centers to hold in place.
5. Turn under hem allowance on one side of each inner piece by folding ½" and then another ½". Press and slipstitch in place.
6. With right sides together, pin the inner two pieces to each side of the large piece. Insert lace if desired at this point. Stitch the seam allowance, adjusting for fit to the album and thickness of batting.
7. Make two small strips hemmed on one side to stitch, and finish the center edges at the ring opening.
8. Turn the cover inside out. By flipping the covers together with the right sides together, you can slip the ends of the cover onto the binder.
9. Glue the frame piece to the front. Glue trim as desired.

Frame piece

1. Cut the photo frame shape from cardboard. Cut another piece without the opening.
2. Trace the frame shape onto the batting and cut.
3. Glue the batting piece onto the front side of the frame piece opening.
4. Cut two frame pieces with opening from fabric, allowing ½" seam allowance.
5. Cut one solid frame piece with ½" seam allowance.
6. With opening fabric pieces right sides together, stitch along the center seam. Snip center edges, turn pieces inside out, and press.

7. Cover the frame front and back by putting the two joined pieces through the center. Smooth them out and glue around the center opening.
8. Trim the edges of the back piece. Glue the seam allowance of the front piece over the back piece.
9. Cover the remaining frame piece with fabric and glue in place, turning the seam allowances to the back.
10. Glue three sides of the backing piece to the front piece with opening. The open side is for inserting the picture. Glue the whole frame piece to the front of the album with the unfinished back side adhered to the album. Trim as desired.

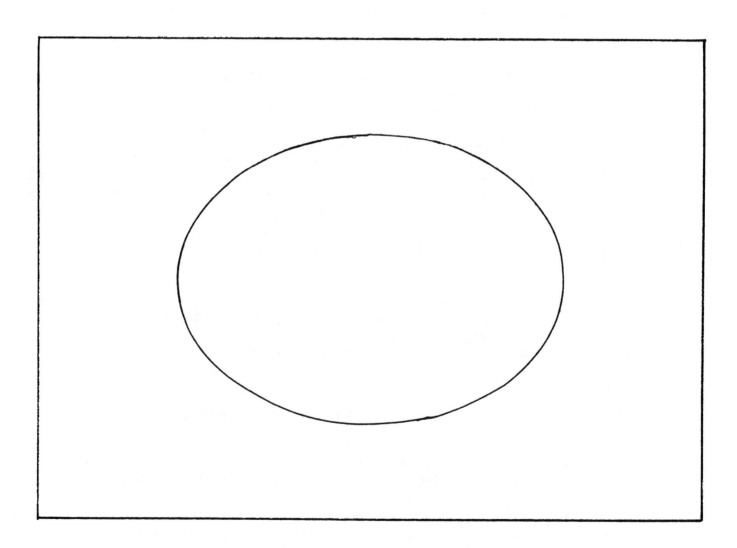

Chapter 14
Successful Ending

How a project is finished separates the novice from the professional. Whether making a quilt, pillow, or garment, it is the small details that make for success. Take time to master some simple techniques for finishing. Try an envelope closure for a pillow. Learn to make your own continuous bias so that your binding is coordinated with your project. Take time to put welting or ruffles in a pillow edge. Learn to miter edges. Try making prairie points for an interesting border. The time you take to add a touch of perfection will be appreciated by others and will make for a successful ending.

Prairie Points

Prairie points make an attractive finished edge for items such as a quilt, skirt, apron, or basket trim.

Directions

1. Cut 4″ squares from fabric.
2. Fold the piece in half on the bias.
3. Fold again on the bias into fourths.
4. Repeat this with all pieces.
5. Insert one piece between another as shown.
6. Baste the raw edges along the right side of a border edge.
7. Stitch a ½″ seam and turn the points down.
8. To superimpose on a project, baste or glue in place and cover the raw edge with braid.

   Decorate a berry basket as follows: Spray paint the basket. Make prairie points to cover the top edge. Glue in place. Finish with ribbon.

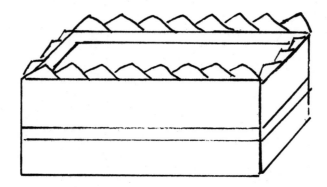

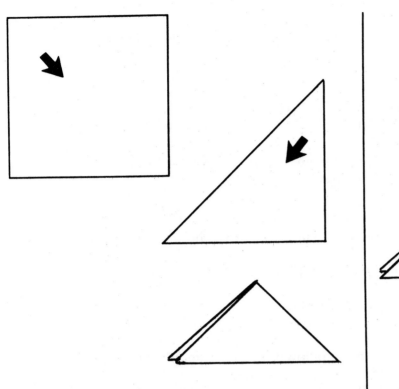

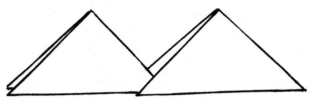

Prairie points arrangement

4" square for prairie points

199

Envelope Closure

Commercial pillow forms come in 8″, 10″, 12″, 14″, 16″, and 18″ sizes. Unless you wish to make your own pillow form, plan a pillow project in commercial pillow sizes.

The envelope closure is a convenient backing for a pillow. It requires no zipper but allows for a pillow form to be removed easily.

Directions

1. Measure your pillow back dimensions by adding one half the pillow width plus 3″ by the length.
   Example: For a 14″ pillow add 7″ plus 3″, making 10″ by 14″ for each back piece.
2. Cut two back pieces of required measurements.
3. Turn under a ½″ seam twice on each piece lengthwise at the center. Hem and slipstitch.
4. Overlap the two pieces, adjusting to the pillow finished width. The overlap should be about 3″ wide. Stitch the overlap.
5. Place the whole backing on the pillow front with right sides together and stitch. Welting or ruffle is added to the front pillow piece before the backing. If using trim, baste in place and then proceed with sewing the front and back.

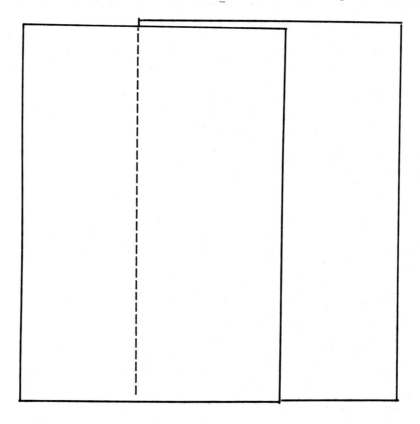

Bound Edges

Quilt binding can be cut along the grain edge if there is enough fabric. To conserve fabric, use the continuous bias method. When planning a quilt, binding should be considered in fabric measurements. A yard of fabric will be needed for binding a double quilt with the continuous bias method. To cut along the grain will take as much as 3 yards.

To bind a quilt with fabric cut along the grain, mark and cut a 4″ wide fabric strip. Fold lengthwise in half. Then fold the doubled strip into thirds. Open and place the doubled raw edges along the quilt front edge. Stitch a ⅝″ seam. Press the binding around the edge. At the back, slipstitch the folded edge. This makes a double binding which wears well.

For binding a garment, either make continuous bias or cut 2″ strips on the bias. Fold the strips in half. Open up and fold each edge to the center fold line, making fourths. Line an edge with the garment edge with right sides together. Stitch the ½″ seam allowance. Turn the folded edge to the back. Press and slipstitch.

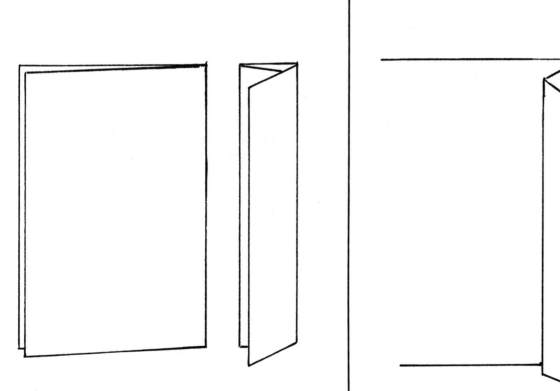

4″ strips for binding quilt. Fold in half once and fold in thirds.

Line right sides together at edge of quilt and stitch. Turn and finish the folded edge by hand.

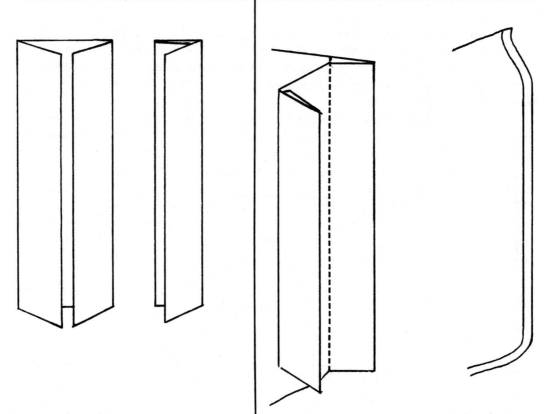

2" strips for garment binding. Press in half, open, and press sides to the center.

Line a raw edge against the garment edge and stitch ½" seam. Turn and stitch folded edge by hand.

Mitered corners are another way of finishing a bound quilt edge.

1. Border strips for the edges will be cut close to the edge.
2. Each edge corner will be pressed flat up and down to make a crease or fold line where you will stitch. Pin the edges together.
3. Trim excess along a ½″ seam line.
4. Stitch the diagonal folded line along pinned edge.
5. Press the seam open. Turn and finish.

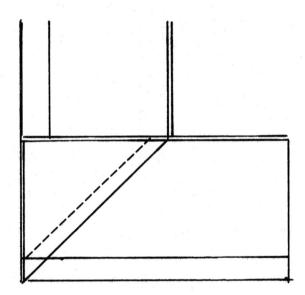

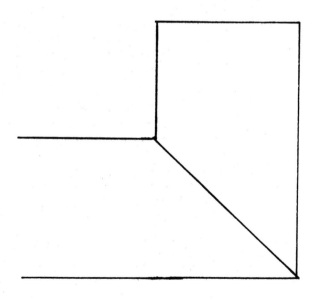

Hanging a Quilt

To hang a quilt for a show requires a sleeve pocket for the back top. Directions are usually included in show entrance information as follows: Cut a piece of fabric which preferably matches your backing fabric in a strip 7″ deep and the width of the quilt. Stitch a small hem at each end. With right sides together, pin and stitch the raw edges of the long side. Turn inside out and baste each long side to the top of the quilt. This will provide a pocket for a display rod to be put through.

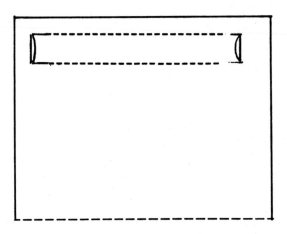